London in detail

London in detail is a unique record of some of the intrinsic details of the architecture and 'street furniture' of the capital: milestones, street names, bollards, street lamps, public seats, drinking fountains, horse troughs, telephone kiosks, pillarboxes, litterbins, railings, gateposts, animals, coalhole covers, manhole covers, fire hydrants, gates, doors, street and house numbers, fanlights and other doorway details, knobs and knockers, bell-pushes, letterboxes, footscrapers, balconies, windows, drainpipes, air vents, chimneys, rooftops, spires, weathervanes, clocks, sculpture on buildings, heads, statues, lettering on buildings, brick patterns, mosaic tiles, cobbles and setts, grilles and gratings, plaques, trade signs, shop fronts, signposts, graffiti and jokes, pub signs and crests of London.

A team of seven specially commissioned photographers took 12,000 photographs, from which 2000 pictures were selected for this book (which originally appeared in hardback as *The London Book* in 1980).

The strength of *London in detail* lies in the fact that not only is it still fascinating to look at, but it has now become an invaluable documentation since the face of London has changed so dramatically since the book's original conception. The reader should, therefore, not be surprised if some of the details included in this book have now disappeared, been replaced, moved to new locations or, alas, been demolished.

As Sir Hugh Casson says in his Foreword the book is 'more like a birdspotter's notebook than a guide – and just as indispensable . . . fun for the reader who, eyes sharpened by the treasures so affectionately listed on these pages, will be able to seek out and enjoy new ones for himself.'

Ian Hessenberg is Senior Lecturer in Photography at the Central School of Art and Design, London, and runs his own photographic practice.

FRONT COVER: Field & Sons, 54 Borough High Street, SE1 (*Andra Nelki*)

BACK COVER: (*top l*) Willis Faber p.l.c., 10 Trinity Square, EC3 (*Susan Greenhill*), (*top centre*) 13 Great Ormond Street, WC1 (before conversion) (*Susan Greenhill*), (*top r*) Shipwrights Arms, 88 Tooley Street, SE1 (*Prunella Bramwell-Davis*); (*bottom l*) Good Shepherd Mission, Mosslea Road, SE20 (*Susan Greenhill*), (*bottom centre*) Young & Co's Brewery Ltd, Ram Brewery, Wandsworth High Street, SW18 (*Andra Nelki*), (*bottom r*) Central Hall, Storey's Gate, SW1 (*Prunella Bramwell-Davis*)

London
in detail

edited by
Ian Hessenberg

Foreword by
Sir Hugh Casson PPRA

John Murray

Editor's Note

To record the details which are so much a part of the character of London, I relied on a team of seven dedicated and self-disciplined photographers. They had to be objective, which in essence meant suppressing all creative and artistic feelings in favour of a purely documentary photograph – this was much more difficult than one might imagine. The brief for each photographer was to record everything of interest within their allotted area, and in order to maintain graphic and comparative imagery all the photographs (with few exceptions) were taken straight on from street level.

There are 6000 miles of streets in London. We covered most of them on foot, bicycle, car and bus looking for suitable material. Over 12,000 suitable photographs were taken from which I selected the 2059 in this book. Every day I see more and more fascinating details which I would have loved to include – sadly the line had to be drawn somewhere. My grateful thanks to the photographers – it *was* worth all their effort and patience.

London was divided into rough geographical areas and assigned to the photographers as follows:

Prunella Bramwell-Davis and Andra Nelki: South London
Peter Fleissig: East End and North London
Susan Greenhill: City and West End
Ian Hessenberg: Kensington, Chelsea and West London
Jessie Ann Matthew: Islington and Hampstead
Mary Spendlove: part of West Hampstead and part of Finchley

Technical details: The cameras used were Pentax and Nikon equipped mainly with telephoto lenses (135/200mm) or zoom lenses with macro facility.

Film: Ilford HP5; Developer: Paterson Acutol FX 14; Prints: Ilfospeed R/C paper.

Originally published 1980 as *The London Book*
Paperback edition first published 1986
by John Murray (Publishers) Ltd, 50 Albemarle Street, London WIX 4BD
Reprinted 1987
© Ian Hessenberg 1980, 1986
Designed by Amanda Lester   Research by Philippa Urmston
Captions by Ian Grant FRIBA, and Philippa Urmston
Photographic printing by Tessa Musgrave
Printed and bound in Great Britain by Hazell Watson & Viney Limited, Aylesbury

British Library Cataloguing in Publication Data

[The London book]. London in detail.
  1. London (England)—Buildings, structures,
  etc.– Pictorial works
  I. Hessenberg, Ian
  729'.09421   NA3544.L6

ISBN 0-7195-4339-8

Foreword
Sir Hugh Casson PPRA

This is a picture book about London . . . not about its familiar streets, parks, squares and monuments but about those details of which all these architectural elements are composed – fanlights and coalholes, bollards and lamp posts, pillarboxes, street signs, domes and door knockers. Such things are not always shown on architects' drawings. Often nobody knows who originally designed them, ordered them or placed them. The variety of messages they carry – portentous or witty, elegant or clumsy, sensible or dotty – is as endless as their materials and the methods by which they have been stamped, hammered, carved, moulded and cast into existence.

Virtually none of them is a masterpiece. Probably few will attract the protection of a preservation order. All are desperately vulnerable to decay, removal or destruction, often for (apparently) the best or most logical reasons. It is the modesty of these objects that places them at risk, reinforcing the growing public view that the 'usefulness' of a building – or a part of a building – should be calculated on other things besides straight architectural merit. Every city needs a proportion of old buildings – unspectacular, shabby homes for people or enterprises that have no need for new construction – and also of old artefacts, signs and gratings and footscrapers and railings which may in some sense have outlived their original purpose but still bring vitality of detail and humanity to the street scene. London, luckily, is still rich in these pieces of outdoor furniture. As a lifelong Londoner I have grown to recognise their importance, to love and cherish them, even to look out for them, for they are so easy to miss or take for granted.

But the fact that they are often small and easily overlooked does not mean they are unimportant. These are the things we meet at eye-level, which we touch or walk upon. They are footnotes to history and evidence of social behaviour. Hand-carved sculpture or carefully built spirelets were normally accepted elements of a building and are evidence of a one-time labour-intensive economy. A coalhole cover reminds us of the complicated paraphernalia of the Victorian domestic scene – housemaids and coal scuttles and smoking chimneys and huge horse-drawn carts with their sharp-smelling sacks and burnished weighing machines. Footscrapers are the relics of muddy streets and crossing sweepers. All such things are clues to our existence, lifelines to identity, signals to recognise and to which we respond.

This makes this fascinating book more like a birdspotter's notebook than a guide – and just as indispensable, both as a valuable record of 'endangered species' and, literally, as an eye-opener to the beauty of detail. It must have been great fun to compile but it will be even more fun for the reader who, eyes sharpened by the treasures so affectionately listed on these pages, will be able to seek out and enjoy new ones for himself.

H. C. April 1986

1 KENSINGTON GORE SW7

1 KENSINGTON COURT W8

EALING COMMON W5

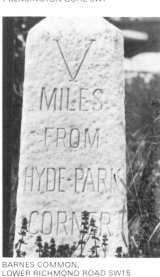

GROVE STREET SE8

BARNES COMMON,
LOWER RICHMOND ROAD SW15

CAREY STREET WC2

689 HARROW ROAD NW10

THE BROADWALK.
KENSINGTON GARDENS W8

YE OLD GATE HOUSE PUB,
HAMPSTEAD LANE AND WEST HILL N6

HARMSWORTH PARK SE1

32 PECKHAM ROAD SE5

214 HIGH STREET W3

'THE LAMB',
LAMBS CONDUIT STREET WC1

FINSBURY PAVEMENT EC2

VESTA ROAD SE4

VESTA ROAD SE4

79 HAVERSTOCK HILL NW3

HIGH LEVEL DRIVE SE26

KENSINGTON GARDENS W8

RUSKIN WALK SE24

MILE END ROAD E1

LEICESTER SQUARE WC2

WILDS RENTS SE1

OFF FIRST STREET SW3

JEWS WALK SE26

WAPPING WALL E1

EATON TERRACE SW1

CHURCH LANE E17

RAILWAY COTTAGES NW10

445 BATTERSEA PARK ROAD SW11

ALIE STREET E1

CLINK STREET SE1

The slang expression 'clink' meaning prison comes from the former Clink Prison on Bankside, which also gave rise to 'on the fiddle' because of the fiddle sign which hung above the prison.

HOLLAND PARK MEWS W11

QUEENS GATE SW7

KINGS ARM YARD EC2

ELECTRIC LANE. S.W.9.

DOWNING STREET SW1

DUKE STREET W1

WEST INDIA DOCK ROAD E14

CAMPDEN HOUSE CLOSE W8

HUNTERS MEADOW S.E.19

DENBIGH MEWS W11

OFF WESTOW STREET SE19

DUNSANY ROAD W14

The area where the order of the Friars of the Holy Cross was founded soon became known as Crutched Friars due to their blue habits with a red cross back and front.

OFF STOCKWELL ROAD SE10

NOW GREAT PETER STREET SW1

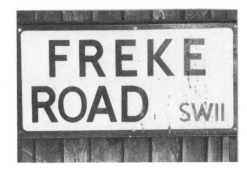

FREKE ROAD SW11

The 'fat boy' represents the sin of gluttony which is said to have caused the Great Fire since it began in Pudding Lane and ended here at Pie Corner.

COCK LANE EC1

STAR STREET W2

BACON'S LANE N1

CLAPHAM COMMON NORTH SIDE SW4

RAILWAY AVENUE SE16

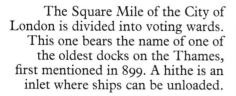

LAURENCE POUNTNEY HILL EC4

The Square Mile of the City of London is divided into voting wards. This one bears the name of one of the oldest docks on the Thames, first mentioned in 899. A hithe is an inlet where ships can be unloaded.

QUEEN VICTORIA STREET EC4

NOBLE STREET EC2

LUDGATE HILL EC4

HOLBORN VIADUCT EC1

SOUTHWARK BRIDGE SE1

VINE STREET EC3

STRAND WC2

HAWLEY STREET NW1

100 WOOD STREET E17

PARK CRESCENT W1

GROVE STREET SE8

ROCHELLE STREET E2

LEICESTER SQUARE WC2

GRACECHURCH STREET EC3

BARLBY ROAD W10

EARSBY STREET W14

CAVENDISH COURT EC3

STRAND WC2

SOUTH MOLTON STREET W1

COMMERCIAL STREET E1

JAMES STREET WC2

LEXHAM WALK W8

39 SOUTHWARK BRIDGE ROAD SE1

Many obsolete cannons were used as bollards in the early nineteenth century, with an oversized cannon ball filling the muzzle.

FOREST HILL STATION SE23

ST ALFEGE PASSAGE SE10

SOMERSET HOUSE, STRAND WC2

MONTPELIER SQUARE SW7

ST PAUL'S CHURCHYARD EC4

BROWNING ROAD E11

MCNEIL ROAD SE5

IMPERIAL WAR MUSEUM,
LAMBETH ROAD SE1

CHESHAM CLOSE SW1

LINCOLN'S INN FIELDS WC2

HOLBORN VIADUCT EC1

When Holborn Viaduct was built in 1869 it provided a much needed improvement in communication across the steep Fleet river valley. The success of the achievement was commemorated by the City in the rich detail of railings, lamps and symbolic sculpture incorporated in the work.

LEYTONSTONE HIGH ROAD E11

13–17 PALL MALL EAST SW1

BARTON STREET SW1

HOLBORN VIADUCT EC1

WINCHESTER MEWS NW3

EARLS COURT ROAD SW5

HYDE PARK W2

WATERLOO PLACE SW1

HAMMERSMITH GARDENS W6

3 MONTPELIER SQUARE SW7

CAMBERWELL REGISTER OFFICE SE5

WESTMINSTER BRIDGE SW1

12 ST ALBAN'S GROVE W8

St Alfege

ST ALFEGE PARISH CHURCH
OF GREENWICH SE10

The four-sided lantern with canted panes and a circular top vent was probably the most widely used of all nineteenth century street lights. It was first illuminated by a fishtail gas burner, then an incandescent gas burner, then in the twentieth century, by electric light.

ROYAL NAVAL COLLEGE,
KING WILLIAM WALK SE10

ASHLEY PLACE SW1

STRAND WC2

LECKY STREET SW7

WEDLAKE STREET W10

PUTNEY BRIDGE SW15

EUSTON GROVE NW1

1 WIMPOLE STREET W1

CHELSEA EMBANKMENT SW3

TOWER BRIDGE E1

23 QUEEN SQUARE WC1

THE MALL SW1

It was only with the advent of electricity that it became practical to point the light source downwards, and this radically affected the design of lamp standards.

55 EBURY STREET SW1

PORTLAND PLACE W1

MARYLEBONE ROAD NW1

DULWICH HAMLET SCHOOL SE21

The twelve-pane glass globe was a very popular form of Victorian gas lantern, and it was mounted on a wide variety of elaborate columns.

YOUNG AND CO,
WANDSWORTH HIGH STREET SW18

BRIDGE ON HORNSEY LANE N6

VICTORIA AND ALBERT MUSEUM,
CROMWELL ROAD SW7

WILTON CRESCENT SW1

PUTNEY BRIDGE SW15

GATES, GREENWICH PARK SE10

WANDSWORTH TOWN HALL SW18

10 TRINITY SQUARE EC3

LAMBETH BRIDGE SW8

HYDE PARK W2

15 HARRINGTON ROAD SW7

7 DILKE STREET SW3

11 THAMES ROAD W4

60 PIMLICO ROAD SW1

7 HARLEY ROAD NW3

11 FITROY ROAD NW1

8 EATON TERRACE SW1

55 PRINCE'S GATE MEWS SW7

THE WINDMILL, CLAPHAM COMMON SW4

CAMBERWELL TOWN HALL,
PECKHAM ROAD SE5

NORWEGIAN CHURCH,
ALBION STREET SE16

THE MALL SW1

18 FINSBURY SQUARE EC2

193 EUSTON ROAD NW1

CROWN LANE GARDENS ESTATE SE27

BUCKINGHAM PALACE, THE MALL SW1

BANK OF ENGLAND.
THREADNEEDLE STREET EC2

446 FULHAM ROAD SW6

IRONMONGERS HALL,
ALDERSGATE STREET EC1

BATTERSEA DISTRICT LIBRARY,
ALTENBURG GARDENS SW11

BATTERSEA DISTRICT LIBRARY,
ALTENBURG GARDENS SW11

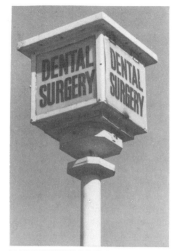

65 BROOMWOOD ROAD SW11

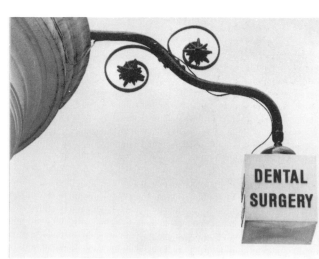

16 TAVISTOCK PLACE WC1

9 CARNABY STREET W1

BRIXTON ROAD SW9

UPPER BELGRAVE STREET SW1

24 HILLGATE STREET W8

HYDE PARK W2

2 LOWER CLAPTON ROAD E5

GARRATT LANE SW18

STATION ROAD SW13

EAST ACTON LANE W3

RUSSELL HOTEL, RUSSELL SQUARE WC1

LAVENDER GARDENS SW11

HIGH STREET
AND GUNNERSBURY LANE W3

THE MALL SW1

THE BRIDGE HOUSE,
BOROUGH ROAD SE1

POST OFFICE COURT EC4

ALBERT EMBANKMENT SE1

BARONS COURT TUBE STATION W14

BATTERSEA RISE SW18

PARLIAMENT SQUARE SW1

105A CRAWFORD STREET W1

ORIEL PLACE NW3

CHALCOT SQUARE NW1

VICTORIA EMBANKMENT WC2

VICTORIA EMBANKMENT EC4

GREENWICH PARK SE10

ALBERT EMBANKMENT SE1

PECKHAM RYE PARK SE22

HORNIMAN GARDENS, LONDON ROAD SE22

STAPLE INN EC4

BISHOPSGATE CHURCHYARD EC2

GOLDERS HILL PARK NW11

HACKNEY ROAD E2

GOLDERS GREEN BUS STATION NW11

FOREST ROAD E17

BRENT CROSS SHOPPING CENTRE NW4

Sir Giles Gilbert Scott designed this cast-iron telephone kiosk in 1926. Those with the narrow panes of glass *left* were his later design which was produced from 1936.

740 HARROW ROAD W10

UPPER THAMES
AND QUEEN STREETS EC4

CHARING CROSS ROAD WC2

REGENTS PARK ROAD NW1

BLYTHE ROAD POST OFFICE W14

SAVOY PLACE WC2

GROSVENOR GARDENS SW1

ST JAMES'S PARK, BIRDCAGE WALK SW1

QUEEN MARY S COLLEGE, MILE END ROAD E1

CLAPTON SQUARE E5

SPANIARDS END NW3

CORNHILL EC3

1886

IN MEMORY
OF
NATHANIEL MONTEFIORE, ESQ.
OF WHOM IT WAS TRULY WRITTEN
HE SOUGHT TO DO THE MAXIMUM OF GOOD
WITH THE MINIMUM OF NOTORIETY.
THIS FOUNTAIN HAS BEEN ERECTED
BY HIS WIFE EMMA MONTEFIORE

ST JAMES'S BERMONDSEY,
CHURCHYARD GARDENS SE16

PIMLICO ROAD SW1

You are reminded to 'replace the cup' at the first metropolitan drinking fountain, unveiled by the daughter of the Archbishop of Canterbury in 1859.

REPLACE THE CUP.

PARISH CHURCH OF THE HOLY SEPULCHRE, HOLBORN VIADUCT EC1

CHURCHYARD RECREATION GROUND,
BERMONDSEY STREET SE1

COMMERCIAL STREET, SPITALFIELDS E1

VICTORIA EMBANKMENT GARDENS WC2

VICTORIA TOWER GARDENS SW1

VICTORIA EMBANKMENT GARDENS WC2

HORNIMAN GARDENS,
LONDON ROAD SE23

DEPTFORD PLAYGROUND,
WATSON STREET SE8

SPENCER PARK SW18

Horse troughs were a most necessary piece of street furniture even as late as the 1930s, when much slow goods transport was still horse-drawn. Older Londoners will vividly remember the queues of carts with their horses waiting for refreshments on hot days.

ST PAUL'S ALLEY EC4

GRAY'S INN SQUARE WC1

MEADWAY NW11

DULWICH PARK SE21

FORTUNE GREEN, WEST END LANE NW6

SOUTH MOLTON STREET W1

VAUXHALL PARK SW8

PORTSOKEN STREET E1

VICTORIA EMBANKMENT GARDENS WC2

THURLOE STREET SW7

SOUTHWARK CATHEDRAL PRECINCT SE1

FARRINGDON ROAD STATION EC1

CLAPTON SQUARE E5

ST KATHARINE'S DOCK E1

CANONBURY ROAD N1

CAVENDISH AVENUE NW8

POSTMANS PARK, KING EDWARD STREET EC1

EUSTON ROAD NW1

KINGSWAY WC2

CAVENDISH COURT EC3

SHEFFIELD STREET WC2

KINGS ROAD SW3

BRITISH MUSEUM WC1

ST BOTOLPH STREET EC3

STRAND WC2

Few pillarboxes remain that are as old as this one with its elegant hexagonal shape and beaded top.

280 KENSINGTON HIGH STREET W8

MEADWAY AND BIGWOOD ROAD NW11

BEDFORD SQUARE WC1

TREVOR SQUARE SW7

DENMARK HILL STATION, SE5

3 HAMPSTEAD LANE N6

GREAT RUSSELL STREET WC1

CHISWELL STREET EC1

ST PAUL'S CHURCHYARD EC4

HOLDEN ROAD N12

FULHAM ROAD
AND NEVILLE TERRACE SW7

MEADWAY AND HAMPSTEAD WAY NW11

OUTSIDE 18,
BATTERSEA PARK ROAD SW8

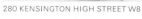

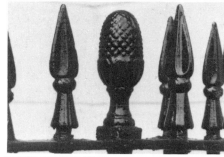

MYDDELTON SQUARE EC1

MYDDELTON SQUARE EC1

40 SUTHERLAND SQUARE SE17

NORWEGIAN CHURCH, ALBION STREET SE16

CHESTER TERRACE, REGENTS PARK NW1

104 KENSINGTON CHURCH STREET W8

CARRICK HOUSE, CALEDONIAN ROAD N7

LEADERS GARDENS, EMBANKMENT SW15

TRINITY CHURCH SQUARE SE1

CAROLINE HOUSE, ASYLUM ROAD SE15

129 OLD CHURCH STREET SW3

ROYAL NAVAL COLLEGE, GREENWICH SE10

19 CHALCOT CRESCENT NW1

MARE STREET E8

71 PALL MALL SW1

75 CARTER STREET SE17

BROMPTON ORATORY SW3

HAMMERSMITH SW13

PUTNEY CEMETERY SW15

179 ARLINGTON ROAD NW1

PUTNEY CEMETERY SW15

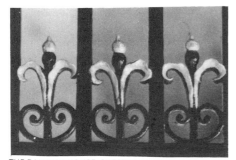

THE RANGERS HOUSE, CHESTERFIELD WALK SE10

15 SAVILE ROW W1

10 BUCKINGHAM GATE SW1

MIDLAND ROAD NW1

DEPTFORD TOWN HALL SE14

The characteristic details of ornamented railings often present an infallible guide to the date of manufacture. Unfortunately, during World War II many railings were removed and melted down to 'help the war effort' and not all have been replaced.

CAMBRIDGE GATE NW1

GRAY'S INN SQUARE WC1

KENILWORTH HOTEL, BLOOMSBURY STREET WC1

70–74 PORTLAND PLACE W1

170 HIGH STREET NW10

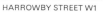
HARROWBY STREET W1

HILLMARTON ROAD N7

Formalised plant forms provided a rich source of design material for railing finials, and many different patterns exist which date from the 'cast-iron years' of the nineteenth century.

THE GROVE N6

OUTER CIRCLE, YORK TERRACE NW1

36 UPPER BELGRAVE STREET SW1

MIDLAND BANK, GOLDERS GREEN NW11

ROYAL HORTICULTURAL SOCIETY, GREYCOAT STREET SW1

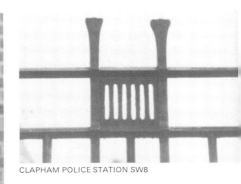

CLAPHAM POLICE STATION SW8

MYLNE STREET EC1

NORTH CAMBERWELL LIBARARY SE5

34 DE VERE GARDENS W8

ROYAL PHYSIC GARDENS SW3

HOLLAND PARK GATES,
KENSINGTON HIGH STREET W8

36 QUEEN ANNES GATE SW1

52 GOWER STREET WC1

14 CHURCH ROAD E10

58 LONGFORD STREET NW1

WANDSWORTH TOWN HALL SW18

42 YORK RISE NW5

9 DAWSON PLACE W2

LAMBETH COUNTY COURT,
CLEAVER STREET SE11

PRUDENTIAL BUILDING, BOUNDARY ROAD E13

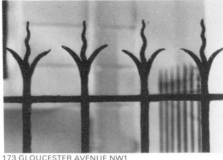

173 GLOUCESTER AVENUE NW1

VENN STREET SW4

3 FLODDEN ROAD SE5

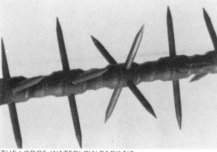

THE LODGE, WATERLOW PARK N6

RESERVOIR, LONSDALE ROAD SW13

308–310 FINCHLEY HIGH ROAD N2

106 CHURCH ROAD E10

CANAL BRIDGE, WEDLAKE STREET W10

HAMMERSMITH CENTRAL LIBRARY W6

HOLLY LODGE, SWAINS LANE N6

8 NEWTON ROAD W2

DULWICH PARK SE21

CORNWALL GARDENS SW7

STOCKWELL GREEN SW9

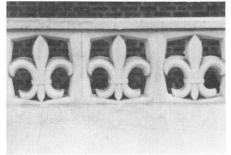
156 KINGS AVENUE SW4

40 BREAKSPEARS ROAD SE4

3 ELM TREE ROAD NW8

EAST ROW W10

PUBLIC LIBRARY, NEW CROSS ROAD SE14

7 ENNISMORE GARDENS MEWS SW7

2 CLAPHAM COMMON NORTH SIDE SW4

EARLSFIELD HOUSE,
SWAFFIELD ROAD SW18

CLARENDON LODGE,
LANSDOWNE RISE W11

ROYAL WATERMAN'S SQUARE, PENGE HIGH STREET SE20

68–70 REGENT'S PARK ROAD NW1

BRITISH HOME AND HOSPITAL
FOR INCURABLES, CROWN LANE SE27

WALSINGHAM SCHOOL, BROOMWOOD ROAD SW11

62–80 HAMPSTEAD WAY NW11

70 ELSWORTHY ROAD NW3

212 SUNSET ROAD SE5

25 EVELINA ROAD SE15

PELHAM CRESCENT SW7

ST NICHOLAS WITH ST LUKE,
DEPTFORD GREEN SE8

185 GLOUCESTER AVENUE NW1

DULWICH PARK, COLLEGE ROAD SE2

NEW CROSS BATHS,
LAURIE GROVE SE14

LANCASTER GATE W2

REGENT'S PARK ROAD NW1

'SUNNYFIELD', WEST HEATH ROAD NW3

HEATHGATE NW11

161 COMMERCIAL STREET E1

HEATHGATE NW11

ST JAMES'S PARISH CHURCH,
WATERLOO ROAD SE1

FOREST HILL SCHOOL,
OAKHURST GARDENS E11

28 ACRE LANE SW2

PEABODY TRUST,
CLAPHAM JUNCTION ESTATE SW11

QUEEN MARY'S GARDEN,
REGENTS PARK NW1

PARISH CHURCH OF ST PAUL, IVELEY ROAD SW4

So long have these notices been painted on the gateposts of the Naval and Military Club in Piccadilly, that the club itself has come to be affectionately known as the 'In and Out'.

NAVAL AND MILITARY CLUB,
PICCADILLY W1

LEADERS GARDENS SW15

WATERLOW PARK N6

HOLLAND PARK GATES,
KENSINGTON HIGH STREET W8

IBIS SPORTS GROUND,
RIVERSIDE DRIVE W4

22 HOOP LANE NW11

OAKFIELD PARK SCHOOL,
THURLOW PARK ROAD SE21

HOLLAND HOUSE, HOLLAND PARK W8

ROYAL WATERMAN'S SQUARE,
PENGE HIGH STREET SE20

WHITE LION STREET N1

ROYAL MEWS,
BUCKINGHAM PALACE ROAD SW1

RIVER THAMES SE1

PALACE GATE,
KENSINGTON GARDENS SW7

BRITISH MUSEUM WC1

490 FULHAM ROAD SW6

WESTMINSTER BRIDGE SW1

149 BOSTON ROAD W7

19 DURAND GARDENS SW9

TRAFALGAR SQUARE WC2

The four lions guarding
Nelson's column, which
were sculpted in 1858–67
by Sir Edwin Landseer,
are probably the best
known of all London's
complement of lions.

50 ELSYNGE ROAD SW18

71 CLAPHAM COMMON
NORTH SIDE SW4

ELEPHANT AND CASTLE, BONDWAY SE1

IMPERIAL COLLEGE TOWER SW7

31 CLEAVER SQUARE SE11

179 NEW KINGS ROAD SW6

SOUTH AFRICAN HOUSE, TRAFALGAR SQUARE WC2

ALBERT MEMORIAL,
KENSINGTON GARDENS SW7

PECKHAM ROAD SE15

IVORY HOUSE, EAST SMITHFIELD E1

CONCERT HALL, CATFORD ROAD SE6

4–5 KING WILLIAM STREET EC4

FLOOD STREET SW3

LONDON CHAMBER OF COMMERCE
AND INDUSTRY CANNON STREET EC4

THE POPPINJAY, FLEET STREET EC4

118 CLAPHAM COMMON
WEST SIDE SW11

16 DAWSON PLACE W2

WATERLOW PARK N6

82 ABBEVILLE ROAD SW4

24 GROSVENOR SQUARE W1

RAF MEMORIAL,
VICTORIA EMBANKMENT WC2

DE VERE HOTEL, DE VERE GARDENS W8

KING WILLIAM STREET EC4

68–70 FENCHURCH STREET EC3

STREATHAM HIGH ROAD SW16

149 HARLEY STREET W1

TATE LIBRARY SW8

VICTORIA EMBANKMENT EC4

ST ANTONY'S FLATS, CHALTON STREET NW1

The lamp globes which line the Thames Embankment like a string of illuminated pearls are supported on magnificent cast-iron standards with intertwined dolphins at their bases. The design dates from the construction of the Embankment by Sir Joseph Bazalgette 1864–70.

68 ST AGNES PLACE SE11

CHURCH OF THE ENGLISH MARTYRS, MITCHAM LANE SW16

29 MOLBURY ROAD W14

ST ERMIN'S HOTEL, CAXTON STREET SW1

BLACKFRIARS BRIDGE EC4

VICTORIA EMBANKMENT GARDENS WC2

HOLBORN VIADUCT EC1

KENSINGTON GARDENS W2

KEW GARDENS, RICHMOND

DULWICH PARK SE21

HOLBORN VIADUCT EC1

LONDON SCHOOL OF HYGIENE
AND TROPICAL MEDICINE, WC1

NATIONAL WESTMINISTER BANK,
VICTORIA STREET SW1

The models of prehistoric animals are an extraordinary survival of the Victorian concern for education. When they were nearly complete in 1853, the scientists in charge and some of their colleagues celebrated the event by dining in the belly of the Iguanodon.

CRYSTAL PALACE PARK SE19

ST GEORGE'S HANOVER SQUARE, GEORGE STREET W1

ST PANCRAS GARDENS NW1

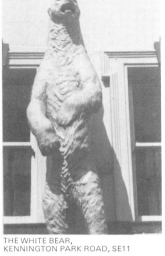

BATTERSEA DOGS' HOME SW8

THE WHITE BEAR, KENNINGTON PARK ROAD, SE11

151 GREYHOUND LANE SW16

46 ST JOHN'S HILL GROVE SW11

3 STAFFORD STREET W1

GOLDSMITHS HALL, FOSTER LANE EC2

SOUTH AFRICA HOUSE, TRAFALGAR SQUARE WC2

CRYSTAL PALACE PARK SE19

14 SOUTHWARK BRIDGE ROAD SE1

352 KINGS ROAD SW3

68 ST AGNES PLACE SE11

'CUTTY SARK', GREENWICH SE10

THE ROEBUCK, GREAT DOVER STREET SE1

26 ST JOHN'S LANE EC1

DEPTFORD PLAYGROUND, WATSON STREET SE8

CALAIS GATE, CORMONT ROAD SE5

PUTNEY HIGH STREET SW15

113 CANNON STREET EC4

2 BEAUCHAMP PLACE SW3

TIGER TAVERN

LOWER THAMES STREET EC3

HENRY FAWCETT INFANT SCHOOL,
BOWLING GREEN STREET SE11

DICK WHITTINGTON'S CAT, HIGHGATE HILL N6

SOUTH AFRICA HOUSE,
TRAFALGAR SQUARE WC2

ALBERT MEMORIAL,
KENSINGTON GARDENS SW7

10 GARFORD STREET E14

PALACE GATE,
KENSINGTON GARDENS SW7

8–9 GILTSPUR STREET EC1

2 SUNNYHILL ROAD SW16

THE WHITE HART,
LOUGHBOROUGH ROAD SE5

57 TUFTON STREET SW1

10 ROSSLYN HILL NW3

BEDFORD PLACE WC1

The London terrace house 'with coal under the pavement and servants in the attics' was described by Robert Furnaux Jordan as 'the most brilliantly functional design'. The coal was supplied to the cellar by tipping it through a circular coal hole, closed when not in use by variously ornamented patent cover plates.

GUILFORD STREET WC1

YORK STREET W1

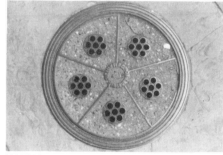

MONTAGUE STREET WC1

GRENVILLE STREET WC1

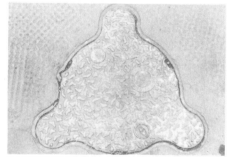

STRAND WC2

GRENVILLE STREET WC1

NASSAU STREET W1

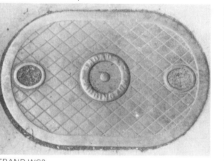

CLEMENTS INN WC2

BERNARD STREET WC1

ALL SAINTS CHURCH, ROSENDALE ROAD SE21

MONTAGUE STREET WC1

WATERLOW PARK N6

BALCOMBE STREET NW1

GOWER STREET WC1

COLBROOKE ROW N1

REGENTS PARK NW1

40 HYDE PARK GATE SW7

COLBROOKE ROW N1

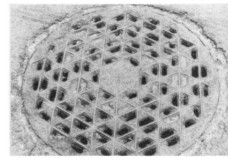

MYDDELTON SQUARE EC1

HARCOURT STREET W1

HAREWOOD AVENUE NW1

126 LOWER RICHMOND ROAD SW15

70 ST AGNES PLACE SE11

DORSET SQUARE NW1

HAREWOOD AVENUE NW1

49 TASMAN ROAD SW9

10 DE VERE GARDENS W8

ROOKSBY STREET N1

ST JOHN'S WOOD HIGH STREET NW8

DORSET SQUARE NW1

BALCOMBE STREET NW1

BALCOMBE STREET NW1

DORSET SQUARE NW1

TURNEY ROAD SE21

113 HUBERT GROVE SW9

REECE MEWS SW7

5 HUBERT GROVE SW9

ALDWYCH WC2

COPTIC STREET WC1

MEADWAY NW11

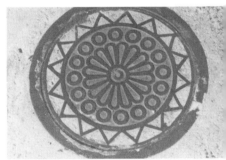

124 LOWER RICHMOND ROAD SW15

110 LANDOR ROAD SW9

EMMOT CLOSE NW11

174 REGENTS PARK ROAD NW1

UNITED REFORMED CHURCH,
UPPER STREET N1

5 BURSTOCK ROAD SW15

QUEEN MARY'S GARDEN, REGENTS PARK NW1

HOLLAND PARK GATES,
KENSINGTON HIGH STREET W8

GREYCOAT HOSPITAL SCHOOL SW1

KENSINGTON HIGH STREET W8

ST JOHNS HILL SW11

28 WANLESS ROAD SE24

30 SUMNER PLACE SW7

DULWICH PARK SE21

HEATHGATE NW11

1 BEVERLEY ROAD W4

47 HALE LANE NW7

44 SYDENHAM HILL SE23

113 DULWICH VILLAGE SE21

22½ DAWSON PLACE W2

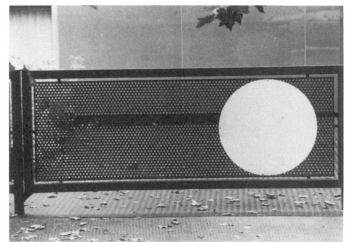

20 CATHCART ROAD SW10

1 RUSKIN WALK SE24

4 MALVERN TERRACE N1

82 RICHMOND AVENUE N1

12 BEDFORD SQUARE WC1

49 CHARLTON TERRACE N1

9 MALVERN TERRACE N1

10 DOWNING STREET SW1

Probably the most famous Georgian doorway in Britain. The house was originally a jerry-built speculation of 1680, which had to be rebuilt in 1723. The door in its present form probably dates from the re-fronting of 1766. Further additions took place in 1825, and the whole place was practically rebuilt in 1962–4 by Raymond Erith.

17 JOHN STREET WC1

82 EATON SQUARE SW1

27 CHARLTON TERRACE N1

27 GROVE TERRACE N6

ST ANDREW'S HOUSE EC4

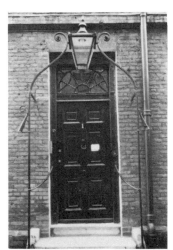

1 AMEN COURT EC4

This is a particularly well-preserved example of a 'well furnished' late eighteenth century (entrance) doorway. It is provided with elegant lamp supports, the snuffers for the link-boys' tarred brands, and the essential boot-scrapers still exist beside the bottom step.

130 HARLEY STREET W1

7 MANSFIELD STREET W1

29A HYDE PARK GATE SW7

23 BEDFORD SQUARE WC1

ST BOTOLPH'S,
ALDGATE HIGH STREET E1

CHELSEA COLLEGE,
MANRESA ROAD SW3

13 BEDFORD GARDENS W8

The main doorway has become a window after successive reconstructions and the conversion of the house into offices. Thomas Gainsborough's occupancy is appropriately celebrated by the palette-holding figure in the central plaque.

SCHOMBERG HOUSE, PALL MALL SW1

39–41 SOUTHWARK BRIDGE ROAD SE1

CASTLETON MANSIONS,
CLAVERING AVENUE SW13

SOUTH AFRICA HOUSE,
TRAFALGAR SQUARE WC2

2 MANSFIELD STREET W1

23–24 GREAT JAMES STREET WC1

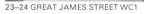

NORTH CAMBERWELL LIBRARY SE5

NORTH CAMBERWELL LIBRARY SE5

24 SOUTHWARK STREET SE1

BATTERSEA TOWN HALL SW11

A typically 'High Victorian' assembly of elements was used to elaborate the entrance to the old Hop Exchange, designed by R H Moore in 1866. The pediment is filled with carved scenes of hop picking.

HOUSES OF PARLIAMENT SW1

13 TOOLEY STREET SE1

TIMBER MERCHANTS, HIGH ROAD N20

WESLEY HALL SE26

PUTNEY SCHOOL OF ART, OXFORD ROAD SW17

DULWICH COLLEGE, COLLEGE ROAD SE21

24 PORTLAND PLACE W1

VINTRY HOUSE, QUEEN STREET PLACE EC4

CENTRAL CRIMINAL COURT OLD BAILEY, EC4

The solemnity and majesty of justice are powerfully symbolised by massive rusticated piers flanking the door; the hooded figure over the pediment gives added emphasis. The Old Bailey was built in 1907 on the site of the even more architecturally terrifying Newgate prison.

CALVARY CHURCH OF GOD IN CHRIST,
FENTIMAN ROAD SW8

LINCOLN'S INN FIELDS WC2

167 ADELAIDE ROAD NW3

Samuel Wyatt was probably the designer of this gateway, round about 1780. He made use of symbolic ornament to enliven his strictly classical composition by introducing crossed anchors in the roundel below the cornice and the traditional bucranium on the keystone to suggest victualling.

33 MONTAGU PLACE W1

39 BEDFORD SQUARE WC1

ROYAL VICTUALLING YARD,
GROVE STREET SE8

Sir Herbert Baker, architect of the Bank, tried to pay homage to his distinguished predecessor Sir John Soane, when he carried out the reconstruction in 1921–37. Despite his efforts at neo-classicism the details on the great bronze doors to the Threadneedle Street entrance have an unmistakably Art Decor look.

BANK OF ENGLAND,
THREADNEEDLE STREET EC2

51 WINDSOR ROAD E7

THE DUKES HEAD, THE PLATT SW15

73 HOLLAND PARK W11

JAMES ALLEN'S GIRLS' SCHOOL,
EAST DULWICH GROVE SE22

SHELL CENTRE SE1

115 LANDOR ROAD SW9

3 TRINITY CRESCENT SW17

47 CLAPHAM HIGH STREET SW4

33 QUEEN SQUARE WC1

162 SIMONDS ROAD E10

LILFORD ROAD SE5

GROVE MANSIONS,
CLAPHAM COMMON NORTH SIDE SW4

AMBASSADORS THEATRE,
TOWER COURT WC2

2A CHURCH LANE E17

41 GREYHOUND HILL NW4

95 HEATH RISE NW3

5 COCHRANE STREET NW8

242 WEST END LANE NW6

63–65 AIREDALE ROAD W4

11–13 CAIRD STREET W10

31 THE CHASE SW4

33–35 BARFETT STREET W10

32 CAMPDEN GROVE W8

8 GASSIOT ROAD SW17

254 VICARAGE ROAD E10

52 CAMPDEN STREET W8

6 CREDITON HILL NW6

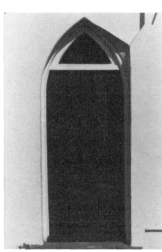

ST PAUL'S SCHOOL
THE RIDGEWAY NW7

24 GROSVENOR CRESCENT MEWS SW1

37 SMITH TERRACE SW3

110 STOCKWELL ROAD SW9

John Ruskin was distressed by the bastardisation of the Venetian Gothic and Romanesque styles that he popularised in such books as *The Stones of Venice*. Yet it is these details which give character to the thousands of middleclass streets that were built in the third quarter of the nineteenth century.

62–64 MARMION ROAD SW11

80 GRAYSHOTT ROAD SW11

160 TURNEY ROAD SE24

21 WESTBURY ROAD N12

8 KNATCHBULL ROAD SE5

STOCKWELL INFANT SCHOOL SW9

97 TORRIANO AVENUE NW5

38 HYDE PARK GARDENS MEWS W2

31 HUBERT GROVE SW9

71 THURLOW PARK ROAD SE21

495 HOLLOWAY ROAD N1

9–11 STATION ROAD SE20

78 SABINE ROAD SW11

1 BEAR LANE SE1

ST SCHOLASTICA, KENNINGHALL ROAD E5

195 SOUTHAMPTON WAY SE5

22 DODDINGTON STREET SE17

39 TURRET GROVE SW4

64 COURTNEY SQUARE SE11

21 CHURCH END E17

28 DULWICH WOOD AVENUE SE19

FREEGROVE HOUSE
FREEGROVE ROAD N7

9 CLARENDON CLOSE W2

ETLOE HOUSE, CHURCH ROAD E10

46 MEADWAY NW11

2 FROGNAL RISE NW3

GAYTON ROAD NW3

4 FROGNAL RISE NW3

1A TREVOR PLACE SW7

A lovely example of 'stockbroker tudor' of around 1925, identified by Osbert Lancaster and beloved by John Betjeman and J M Richards. After many years during which the style invited total contempt, its whimsical charm and 'period' character are now being re-assessed.

6 MEADWAY NW11

2 DE VERE COTTAGES W8

ENDELL STREET WC2

10 CONSTABLE CLOSE NW11

113 FROGNAL NW3

HAMMERS LANE NW7

9–15 OXFORD STREET W1

13 HOBART PLACE SW1

6 GOLDEN SQUARE W1

3 BUCKINGHAM GATE SW1

28 ST JOHN'S LANE EC1

11 TUFTON STREET SW1

91 SHAFTESBURY AVENUE W1

24 PORTLAND PLACE W1

52 MARK LANE EC3

70 ROUPELL STREET SE1

The importance of hanging signs began to decline as soon as street numbering became customary. Traditionally they should carry some kind of symbol of the building or trade whose presence they announce.

3A SEYMOUR WALK SW10

37–60 CAMPDEN HILL ROAD W8

14A ST CROSS STREET EC1

76 HIGH STREET E17

42 THEOBALDS ROAD WC1

459 KINGS ROAD SW3

A particularly attractive Victorian signwriting technique required numbers or letters to be incised into a board; they were then gilded and the whole was set behind protective glass.

344 CALEDONIAN ROAD N1

13 BEDFORD GARDENS W8

53 CHARTERHOUSE STREET EC1

32 RUSSELL ROAD W14

20 CAMBERWELL CHURCH STREET SE5

79 LONG ACRE WC2

50 KINGSLEY WAY N2

8–10 CHURCH END NW4

163 ROSENDALE ROAD SE21

161 COMMERCIAL STREET E1

2A CHURCH LANE E17

12 SPANIARDS CLOSE NW11

16 EDEN ROAD E17

46 BLOOMSBURY STREET WC1

87½ BISHOP'S WAY E2

1 VINTNERS' PLACE EC4

58 GLOUCESTER ROAD SW7

84 CAMPDEN STREET W8

71 GRAY'S INN ROAD WC1

9 ST JAMES'S SQUARE SW1

Over the elegantly painted number on the lamp stand there is still the snuffer, into which the link-boys used to extinguish their tar-covered brands after escorting visitors through unlit streets.

CLERKENWELL ROAD EC1

406 STRAND WC2

16 ST MARTIN'S-LE-GRAND EC1

3 STONE BUILDINGS
LINCOLN'S INN, WC2

81 BELSIZE PARK GARDENS NW3

60 DOLBEN STREET SE1

9 BEDFORD ROW WC1

5 HOLLAND STREET W8

2 LAUREL WAY N20

90 BOROUGH HIGH STREET SE1

6 COTMAN CLOSE NW11

3 GREAT COLLEGE STREET SW1

GREY CLOSE NW11

354 EAST STREET SE17

The semi-circular window over the solid front door used by Georgian builders to light the hallway behind, gave endless opportunities for charming ornamentation. Unfortunately many were damaged during the war, and as in these two examples their glazing bars have never been correctly restored.

62 MYDDELTON SQUARE EC1

60 MYDDELTON SQUARE EC1

19 BEWDLEY STREET N1

22 BEWDLEY STREET N1

The slender, radiating glazing bars, often made in wrought iron tee-section with lead enrichment, immediately suggest the 'fan' from which fanlights take their name.

CHURCH ROW NW3

CANONBURY LANE N1

BARNSBURY STREET N1

Occasionally a late Georgian fanlight might be made in the early eighteenth century style, with thick wood glazing bars and solid ends to the fan-shaped panes, though usually it is safe to say that this type was out of fashion in London by 1750.

VINCENT TERRACE N1

52 DUNCAN TERRACE N1

25 CHARLTON TERRACE N1

The larger the fanlight, the greater degree of elaboration was possible. An intermediate band punctuated by rosettes could be incorporated, with an outer range of swag-shaped bars at the wide end of each division.

81 AMWELL STREET EC1

CANONBURY SQUARE N1

50 CHARLTON TERRACE N1

71 AMWELL STREET EC1

A later type of semi-circular fanlight often had a circular pane in the centre (requiring a non-radiating arrangement of adjacent panes) and it was intended that the house number should be painted on it.

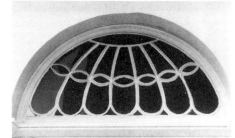
66 INGLEBERT STREET EC1

22 COLLEGE CROSS N1

3 LINCOLN'S INN FIELDS WC2

23 DUNCAN TERRACE N1

The centre panes of fanlights were often subsequently fitted with gas lanterns, to light the front steps, but they were usually carefully designed to fit sympathetically into the available space.

30 COLEBROOKE ROW N1

3 JOHN STREET WC1

8 MYLNE STREET EC1

50 YORK STREET W1

59 MYDDELTON SQUARE EC1

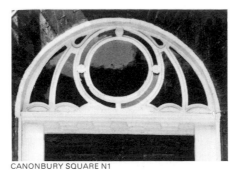

CANONBURY SQUARE N1

34 GREAT JAMES STREET WC1

BARNSBURY STREET N1

CANONBURY SQUARE N1

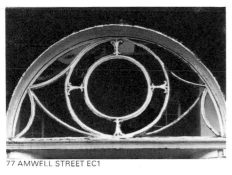

77 AMWELL STREET EC1

40 MYDDELTON SQUARE EC1

3 COLEBROOKE ROW N1

42 CRUTCHED FRIARS EC3

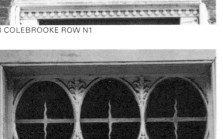

BEDFORD ROW WC1

47 BALCOMBE STREET NW1

BEWDLEY STREET N1

160 CLOUDESLEY ROAD N1

82 AMWELL STREET EC1

1 RIPPLEVALE GROVE N1

14 ERSKINE HILL NW11

48 PORTLAND PLACE W1

LLOYDS BANK, HOLBORN CIRCUS EC1

1 KEATS GROVE NW3

47 ST JOHNS WOOD HIGH STREET NW8

27 CHARLTON TERRACE N1

CHURCH HOUSE, CHURCH END NW4

Not a fanlight but a shell-hood, it was a feature much used by the early Georgians for emphasising a doorway and affording protection from the weather. The idea was enthusiastically revived at the end of the nineteenth century, and by Edwardian architects from whose period this example dates.

NORTH DULWICH STATION SE24

3 GRAY'S INN PLACE WC1

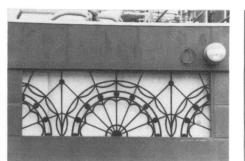

113 HATTON GARDEN EC1

52 GRAFTON WAY W1

13 SOUTHWARK BRIDGE ROAD SE1

8 ST ANDREWS HILL EC4

THE PIED BULL, 496 STREATHAM HIGH ROAD SW16

WATERLOO STATION SE1

Perhaps the ultimate in fanlights, the huge window over the entrance to Waterloo Station poignantly suggests the pride and importance of the railways in the early years of the twentieth century. The station's completion in 1922 allowed the names of the Allies in World War I to be carved on the cartouches which enrich the face of the arch.

10 FERNDALE ROAD SW4

RANGERS HOUSE, CHESTERFIELD WALK SE10

VINTNERS HALL, UPPER THAMES STREET EC4

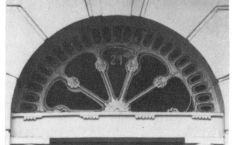

21 MONTAGU SQUARE W1

32 SACKVILLE STREET W1

25 CHURCH ROW NW3

The keystone is traditionally the stone without which the arch would fall, and its ornamentation serves to emphasise its important function. Carved faces, plant forms, crests, rustication: all have been used to draw attention to this vital structural element.

2 DULWICH WOOD AVENUE SE19

WELLINGTON BUILDINGS, GATLIFF ROAD SW1

9 ILCHESTER PLACE W14

WEST INDIA DOCK ROAD E14

14 SLOANE STREET SW1

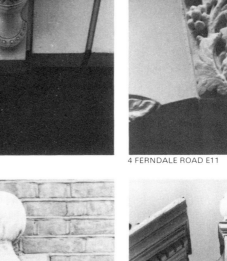

4 FERNDALE ROAD E11

MIDDLESEX POLYTECHNIC, THE BURROUGHS NW4

6 WADHAM GARDENS NW3

1 LYMINGTON ROAD NW6

WALWORTH ROAD SE17

WALWORTH ROAD SE17

10 BUCKINGHAM PLACE SW1

11–12 HOBART PLACE SW1

THE EAGLE, BROOK DRIVE SE11

15 HATHERLEY STREET E17

KING STREET SE1

2 CHEYNE ROW SW3

2A WEIMAR ROAD SW15

12 CLAPHAM COMMON SOUTH SIDE SW4

425 NEW KINGS ROAD SW6

LOWER TERRACE NW3

8 BUCKINGHAM PLACE SW1

HARRODS, KNIGHTSBRIDGE SW1

13–24 CHEYNE WALK SW3

THE COUNTY HALL SE1

327A MILE END ROAD E1

ALLEYN PARK SE21

ALBANY ROAD SE5

97 RIVERSDALE ROAD N5

THE SWAN, DEPTFORD HIGH STREET SE8

POND SQUARE N6

ORFORD ROAD E17

DULWICH COLLEGE, BURBAGE ROAD SE21

114 CHICHELE ROAD NW2

ROSSETTI GARDEN MANSIONS, ST LOO AVENUE SW3

HAMMERSMITH BROADWAY W6

58 BUCKINGHAM GATE SW1

WEST END LANE NW6

9 ROSSLYN HILL NW3

BARCLAYS BANK, ESSEX ROAD N1

WATER LANE E15

HERNE HILL ROAD SE24

CROWN COURT

SWAN STREET SE1

TWININGS

216 STRAND WC2

WOLSELEY STREET SE1

WANDSWORTH TOWN HALL SW18

145 CAMBERWELL ROAD SE5

Above A particularly good example of the type of wrought iron, lead and glass fanlight that was a standard feature in the speculatively built terraces that began to line the main roads out of London in the early nineteenth century.

103 THE CHASE SW4

1 HONEYBOURNE ROAD NW6

1 HEATHGATE NW11

25 ELM TREE ROAD NW8

122 ELGIN CRESCENT W11

148 HORNSEY LANE N6

27 PETHERTON ROAD N5

Unusual inventiveness inspired the designer to form a porch by joining several metal fanlight frames together and supporting them on slender wrought iron members. It was in this house that I K Brunel the great engineer met and courted his wife Mary Horsley at her father's musical evenings.

128 KENSINGTON CHURCH STREET W8

465 CALEDONIAN ROAD N7

4 ATHERDEN ROAD E5

26 CROWNDALE ROAD NW1

149–151 DRAKEFELL ROAD SE4

AGAMEMNON ROAD NW6

AGAMEMNON ROAD NW6

HACKNEY EMPIRE, MARE STREET E8

19–24 ROWHILL ROAD E5

Sunrays in stained glass were immensely popular as panels in front doors during the 1920s and 1930s, though it could well be that this example even dates from after 1945.

3A BARCLAY ROAD E11

162 SIMONDS ROAD E10

115 TURNEY ROAD SE24

32 BROWNING ROAD E11

72 WOODSIDE PARK ROAD N12

CHERTSEY HOUSE, ARNOLD CIRCUS E2

94 HARLEY STREET W1

2 BEDFORD ROW WC1

113 OXFORD STREET W1

34 BEDFORD ROW WC1

THE LONDON LIFE ASSOCIATION
LINCOLNS INN FIELDS WC2

78 AMWELL STREET EC1

10 MILNER STREET SW3

OFFORD ROAD N1

68 KING WILLIAM STREET EC4

20 GREAT CHAPEL STREET W1

22A AVONMORE ROAD W14

29 LINCOLN'S INN FIELDS WC2

MALAYSIA HOUSE,
TRAFALGAR SQUARE WC2

17 DYLWAYS SE5

35 ESSEX STREET WC2

13 ST MARY'S WALK SE11

BLOOMSBURY STREET WC1

WAX CHANDLERS HALL
GRESHAM STREET EC2

37 KING STREET WC2

51 NEW CAVENDISH STREET W1

MOORGATE HALL EC2

1 SUTTON PLACE E9

53 SIDMOUTH STREET WC1

17 OLD BARRACK YARD SW1

80 ST MARTIN'S LANE WC2

37 DORSET ROAD SW8

59 PORTLAND PLACE W1

ST JOHN'S GATE
ST JOHN'S LANE EC1

104 TORRIANO AVENUE NW5

22 WOODSIDE GROVE N12

82 AMWELL STREET EC1

32 BEDFORD SQUARE WC1

TRINITY HOUSE,
SAVAGE GARDENS ENTRANCE EC3

66 BREWER STREET W1

36 CANONBURY SQUARE N1

3 STEDHAM MANSIONS,
COPTIC STREET WC1

75 PORTLAND PLACE W1

70 ROUPELL STREET SE1

14 ESSEX STREET WC2

113 HARLEY STREET W1

A hand holding a wreath was a very common form of knocker during the neo-classical period, and most examples date from about 1790 to 1840.

ESSEX STREET WC2

51 GOWER STREET WC1

8 LORD NORTH STREET SW1

12 NEW BOND STREET W1

ST PETER'S (VAUXHALL), KENNINGTON LANE SE11

Strap hinges, based on medieval patterns, were assiduously produced by all the Gothic Revival architects, and John Loughborough Pearson designed this beautiful example in 1865.

SOUTHWARK CATHEDRAL SE1

THE WINDMILL, CLAPHAM COMMON SW4

8 BATTERSEA PARK ROAD SW11

ST WILFRIDS CHURCH, LORRIMORE ROAD SE17

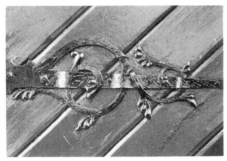

WESTMINSTER BRIDGE SW1

6 MEADWAY NW11

ST WILFRIDS CHURCH, LORRIMORE ROAD SE17

OUR LADY OF THE ROSARY, BRIXTON ROAD SW9

CHURCH OF THE ENGLISH MARTYRS, MITCHAM LANE SW16

10 TRINITY SQUARE EC3

80 ST MARTIN'S LANE WC2

SOUTHWARK CATHEDRAL SE1

ST MARY, CHURCH END E17

14 HENRIETTA STREET WC2

1 CHESHAM CLOSE SW1

243 OLD BROMPTON ROAD SW5

8 EATON TERRACE SW1

WINDMILL THEATRE W1

BIRDCAGE WALK SW1

11–20 CHALLONER ROAD W14

YOUNG'S BREWERY,
WANDSWORTH HIGH STREET SW18

2 FIELD COURT, GRAY'S INN WC1

2 FIELD COURT, GRAY'S INN WC1

12 QUEEN SQUARE WC1

43 BEDFORD SQUARE WC1

1 BEAR LANE SE1

20 ST SWITHIN'S LANE EC4

3 HOLLY MOUNT NW3

IRONMONGERS HALL
ALDERSGATE STREET EC1

11 HARCOURT STREET W1

ST JOHN AND ST ELIZABETH HOSPITAL,
CIRCUS ROAD NW8

AFRICA HOUSE, GATE STREET WC2

21 BROMPTON SQUARE SW3

23 BEDFORD SQUARE WC1

9 GALEN PLACE WC1

LODGE, PUTNEY CEMETERY SW15

8 ADDISON ROAD W14

ST JOHN'S CHURCHYARD, MARE STREET E8

SOUTH LAMBETH ROAD SW8

13 GREAT ORMOND STREET WC1

10 DE VERE GARDENS W8

37 LEWISHAM WAY SE14

105 HUBERT GROVE SW9

10 THEED STREET SE1

469 NEW CROSS ROAD SE14

PORTUGAL STREET WC2

MONKWELL SQUARE EC2

25 HEYFORD AVENUE SW8

HACKNEY EMPIRE, MARE STREET E8

NEW CROSS ROAD SE14

103 BISHOP'S WAY E2

17 HEYFORD AVENUE SW8

23 BEDFORD SQUARE WC1

VANE HOUSE SW1

93 EATON PLACE SW1

1 LIVERPOOL GROVE SE17

12 SHERWOOD STREET N20

66 SYDENHAM ROAD SE26

WOODGRANGE HALL, WOODSIDE GRANGE ROAD N12

PARRY METALS, LASSELL STREET SE10

3 ELM TREE ROAD NW8

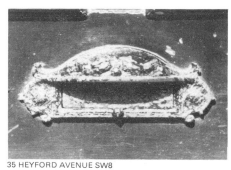

35 HEYFORD AVENUE SW8

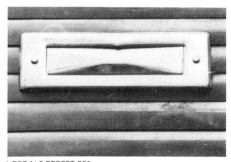

1 BEDALE STREET SE1

43 NORTH STREET SW4

'CONWAY HOUSE', EMMOT CLOSE NW11

GOLDSMITHS HALL, FOSTER LANE EC2

ST PAUL'S CHURCH, THE RIDGEWAY NW7

2 CHEYNE ROW SW3

12 BLENHEIM ROAD NW8

75 CHURCH ROAD E10

36A ELVASTON PLACE SW7

SOUTHWARK CATHEDRAL SE1

THE ROYAL EXCHANGE, THREADNEEDLE STREET EC2

30 CHESTER STREET SW1

MIDDLE TEMPLE EC4

1 HOLLY MOUNT NW3

10 DEVONSHIRE PLACE W1

EDWARD ALLEYN HOUSE, COLLEGE ROAD SE21

7 HANOVER TERRACE NW1

28 MEADWAY NW11

CENTRAL SCHOOL OF ART AND DESIGN,
SOUTHAMPTON ROW WC1

37 BEDFORD PLACE WC1

ST JOHN'S, LEYTONSTONE HIGH ROAD E11

8 DEVONSHIRE PLACE W1

32 BEDFORD SQUARE WC1

42 HIGHGATE HIGH STREET N6

FOREIGN AND COMMONWEALTH OFFICE,
DOWNING STREET SW1

SALVATION ARMY, GARFORD STREET E14

HOLBORN TOWN HALL WC1

MIDDLE TEMPLE EC4

55 BEDFORD ROAD SW4

UNITY HOUSE, EUSTON ROAD NW1

16 LYTTON CLOSE N2

RUSSELL HOTEL WC1

MALL CHAMBERS, KENSINGTON MALL W8

154 GLOUCESTER ROAD SW7

DIGBY MANSIONS, LOWER MALL W6

1 HYDE PARK GATE SW7

RAILWAY TAVERN, BATTERSEA RISE SW11

9–27 FITZGEORGE AVENUE W14

19 PORTLAND PLACE W1

BRIXTON TOWN HALL SW2

DEPTFORD TOWN HALL SE14

48 PORTLAND PLACE W1

29 LINCOLN'S INN FIELDS WC2

5 OLD BARRACK YARD SW1

14 PRINCE ALBERT ROAD NW1

21 MANCHESTER SQUARE W1

LONDON PALLADIUM W1

57 PALL MALL SW1

LLOYDS BANK, FLEET STREET EC4

WHITE HALL HOTEL, BLOOMSBURY SQUARE WC1

94 PARK LANE W1

62 PIMLICO ROAD SW1

99 REGENTS PARK ROAD NW1

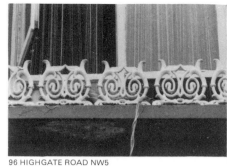

96 HIGHGATE ROAD NW5

OAKLEY SQUARE NW1

27 NORTHWAY NW11

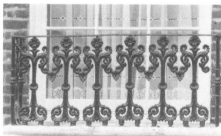

54 ST MARTIN'S LANE WC2

52 GOWER STREET WC1

22 ENGLEFIELD ROAD N1

DE BEAUVOIR ROAD N1

499 HACKNEY ROAD E2

261 REGENT STREET W1

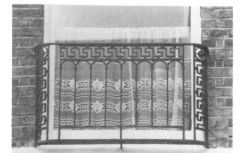

53 DOUGHTY STREET WC1

104 CROUCH HILL N8

WESTBOURNE ROAD N7

ARGAR ROAD N1

79 OFFORD ROAD N1

NEXT TO 98, CHOUMERT ROAD SE15

69 GROSVENOR STREET W1

122 GLOUCESTER ROAD SW7

21 COLLEGE CROSS N1

89 DULWICH VILLAGE SE21

7 CLARENCE PLACE E5

25 ELM TREE ROAD NW8

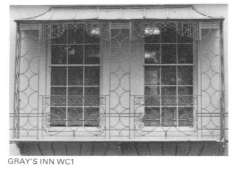

GRAY'S INN WC1

It was a very common practice to protect the balcony and shade the windows with elegantly curved zinc hoods, and these were usually supported on a delicate lacework of wrought or cast iron.

21 BLOOMSBURY SQUARE WC1

WESTMORLAND HOUSE, REGENT STREET W1

16A WILTON STREET SW1

7 CATHCART ROAD SW10

70 MYDDELTON SQUARE EC1

The limitation in sizes of glass available during the eighteenth and early nineteenth centuries required that windows be divided by glazing bars. The introduction of fancifully-shaped bars turned this limitation to decorative use.

19 RIPPLEVALE GROVE N1

25 BEWDLEY STREET N1

11 LISTON ROAD SW4

56 PEMBRIDGE ROAD W11

1 ENNISMORE STREET SW7

LINCOLN'S INN, SERLE STREET WC2

66 KINNERTON STREET SW1

6 STANHOPE PLACE W2

KENTON ARMS, KENTON ROAD E9

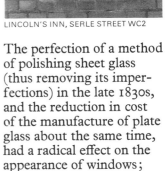

The perfection of a method of polishing sheet glass (thus removing its imperfections) in the late 1830s, and the reduction in cost of the manufacture of plate glass about the same time, had a radical effect on the appearance of windows; glazing bars virtually disappeared for fifty years.

DULWICH COLLEGE, COLLEGE ROAD SE21

20 BUCKINGHAM GATE SW1

By the end of the nineteenth century the craze for large sheets of plain glass in windows had died, and glazing bars were reintroduced in many new buildings purely for aesthetic or romantic effect.

36 ST MARTIN'S LANE WC2

95 BOND STREET W1

170 REGENT STREET W1

THE WHITE LION, PUTNEY HIGH STREET SW15

FEATHERS PUB, BROADWAY SW1

SHIPWRIGHTS ARMS,
TOOLEY STREET SE1

161-165 GREENWICH HIGH ROAD SE10

10 LADBROKE GARDENS W11

ST PANCRAS STATION NW1

46 PARK LANE W1

THE CEDARS, SYDENHAM HILL SE26

25 CHICHELE ROAD NW2

356 GRAY'S INN ROAD WC1

28 ST JAMES'S STREET SW1

45 HOLLYWOOD ROAD SW10

HOUSES OF PARLIAMENT SW1

DENMARK ARMS, BARKING ROAD E6

46-54 GREAT TITCHFIELD STREET W1

26 SOHO SQUARE W1

THE FRENCH INSTITUTE, QUEENSBERRY PLACE SW7

CHRIST CHURCH, BRIXTON ROAD SW9

THE QUEENS',
REGENTS PARK ROAD NW1

23 RUSHEY GREEN SE6

358 KENNINGTON LANE SE11

THE ENTERPRISE, CROGSLAND ROAD NW1

11-13 NEW CROSS ROAD SE14

THE ALBERT, VICTORIA STREET SW1   BARNSBURY STREET N1

2A CHURCH LANE E17

96 CORNWALL GARDENS SW7

1 VESTRY ROAD E17

43 CLAPHAM COMMON NORTH SIDE SW4

James Knowles, who designed this house in 1860, 'signed' nearly all his buildings with similar panels of perforated foliage carving under the heads of the windows.

ST BARTHOLOMEW THE GREAT, WEST SMITHFIELD EC1

BATTERSEA LENDING LIBRARY SW11

8 AVONMORE ROAD W14

39 HYDE PARK GARDENS MEWS W2

HORSE GUARDS ROAD SW1

56 HOLLAND PARK AVENUE W11

WHEATSHEAF, WINTHROP STREET E1

86 PORTOBELLO ROAD W11

WAPPING HIGH STREET E1

The ornamentation of walls with trellis to give *trompe l'oeil* architectural effects was first introduced in France in the late seventeenth century. In this example, on a house built by Oliver Hill in the 1930s, the trellis has been cunningly fitted into a 'blind' window opening.

WILBRAHAM HOUSE,
D'OYLEY STREET SW1

17 CHELSEA EMBANKMENT SW3

27 THE CHASE SW4

61 OXFORD STREET W1

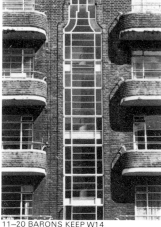

839 HIGH ROAD N12

11–20 BARONS KEEP W14

81 FULHAM ROAD SW3

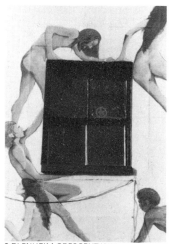

2 BLENHEIM CRESCENT W11

25 ELM TREE ROAD NW8

41 LAVENDER GARDENS SW11

7 AUBREY ROAD W8

111–113 ELGIN CRESCENT W11

WATSON ROAD SE8

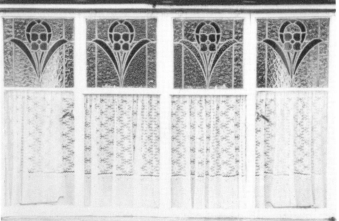

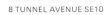

8 TUNNEL AVENUE SE10

Panels of coloured glass in
the upper lights of windows
became popular in the
1870s Arts and Crafts
movement houses, and
remained so until the 1930s.

14 TUNNEL AVENUE SE10

PENGE EAST STATION,
STATION ROAD SE20

48 EATON MEWS NORTH SW1

TOWN HALL PARADE, BRIXTON HILL SW2

12 LANSDOWNE ROAD W11

The protective boxes that the Victorians fitted to their windows to protect external canvas sunblinds have usually survived long after the blinds themselves have rotted and been removed.

34 THURLOW PARK ROAD SE21

THE GOLDEN LION, DENMARK HILL SE5

CANONBURY LANE N1

GREEN ASH, CHISWICK MALL W4

80 HIGHGATE WEST HILL N6

25 WANLESS ROAD SE24

61 DAVIES STREET W1

2 CAMPDEN HOUSE CLOSE W8

21–22 CHEYNE PLACE SW3

170–178 OXFORD STREET W1

Oeil de boeuf or bull's-eye windows were great favourites with French seventeenth and eighteenth century architects like Mansard and Gabriel. This one is treated in a thoroughly French manner, with a carved stone swag beneath to give it emphasis.

1 STATION PARADE NW2

16 ENNISMORE GARDENS MEWS SW7

LEWISHAM CORONERS COURT, LADYWELL ROAD SE13

10 SHELDON ROAD NW2

58 MEADWAY NW11

SOCIAL SERVICES DEPARTMENT, ORFORD ROAD E17

THORNHILL ROAD N1

FRASER HOUSE, ALBION AVENUE SW8

BUSHNELL AND ELMBOURNE ROADS SW17

24 GODFREY STREET SW3

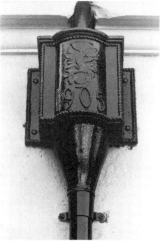

MILL HILL SCHOOL, THE RIDGEWAY NW7

IRONMONGERS HALL,
ALDERSGATE STREET EC1

GRAY'S INN SQUARE WC1

170–178 OXFORD STREET W1

INGLETON HOUSE, RECTORY GROVE SW4

WALTHAM FOREST TOWN HALL E17

The seventeenth and
early eighteenth century
practice of ornamenting
rainwater heads was
enthusiastically revived in
the late nineteenth and
early twentieth centuries.

ALMSHOUSES, CHURCH ROAD E10

IRONMONGERS HALL,
ALDERSGATE STREET EC1

ST PETER OF WALWORTH,
LIVERPOOL GROVE SE17

ST MATTHEW'S CHAPEL,
GREAT PETER STREET SW1

ST PAUL'S CHURCH,
THE RIDGEWAY NW7

149 TIVOLI ROAD SE27

EARLS COURT GARDENS
POST OFFICE SW5

BEVERLEY ROAD W4

WESTMINSTER CATHEDRAL,
AMBROSDEAN AVENUE SW1

36 MEADWAY NW11

THE LONDON STEAKHOUSE,
DULWICH VILLAGE SE21

3 DEAN'S YARD,
GREAT SMITH STREET SW1

ST MARY, CHURCH END NW4

BATTERSEA PUMPING STATION SW8

4 GRAFTON STREET W1

CAMBERWELL SCHOOL OF ARTS
AND CRAFTS, PECKHAM ROAD SE15

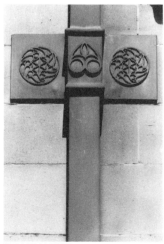

46 PARK LANE W1

BATTERSEA PUBLIC LIBRARY SW11

4 COWLEY STREET SW1

22 MEADWAY NW11

112 KENSINGTON HIGH STREET W8

CHILTERN STREET W1

INNER TEMPLE EC4

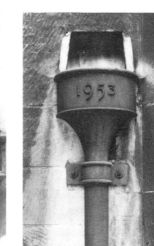

12 QUEEN SQUARE WC1

THE TEMPLE CHURCH,
INNER TEMPLE EC4

359–361 EUSTON ROAD W1

FORMER JEWS HOSPITAL, KNIGHTS HILL SE27

LIBERTY'S,
GREAT MARLBOROUGH STREET W1

The rear part of Liberty's building, which most tourists fondly believe to be an Elizabethan half-timber survival, was in fact built in 1924, using salvaged timbers from two nineteenth century battleships, HMS *Hindustan* and HMS *Impregnable*.

Fresh-air inlets were intended to prevent the vacuums which can occur in sewage systems. They were provided with a mica flap behind the grille which swung back as the pressure inside dropped and then closed when it equalised so that drainage smells could not escape.

13 PETERSHAM PLACE W8

3 ENNISMORE MEWS SW7

5 HILLSLEIGH ROAD W8

38 QUEENS GATE MEWS W8

9 PETERSHAM MEWS SW7

15 QUEENSBERRY WAY SW7

10 ENNISMORE MEWS SW7

16 PRINCE'S GATE MEWS SW7

18 PRINCE'S GATE MEWS SW7

9 PRINCE'S GATE MEWS SW7

44 QUEEN'S GATE MEWS W8

BANK BUILDINGS,
BALHAM STATION ROAD SW12

BANK BUILDINGS,
BALHAM STATION ROAD SW12

LAMBOURNE ROAD SW4

1 HOFLAND ROAD W14

42 BROOK STREET W1

THE DUKE OF CLARENCE,
VAUXHALL BRIDGE ROAD SW1

WEST DULWICH STATION SE21

HOLLY VILLAGE, SWAINS LANE N6

BATTERSEA POWER STATION SW8

Battersea Power Station,
given an expressionist
brick cladding by Sir Giles
Gilbert Scott in 1934, was
considered very remarkable
at the time. It could have
been such chimneys that
gave rise to the remark
'Power stations are the
cathedrals of the
twentieth century'.

LODGE TO BELAIR HOUSE,
BELAIR PARK SE21

HEATHGATE NW11

44–52 WATERLOO GARDENS E2

49 DARTMOUTH ROAD SE23

2 FLASK COTTAGES NW3

CORMONT ROAD SE5

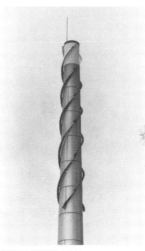

NEWHAM TOWN HALL,
91 THE GROVE E15

14 UPPER BELGRAVE STREET SW1

1 PEMBRIDGE PLACE W2

NEWICK ROAD E5

J AND B ART METAL,
STONEY LANE SE19

60 MILLMAN STREET WC1

DENMARK HILL STATION SE5

DENMARK MANSIONS,
COLDHARBOUR LANE SE5

THE LODGE, WATERLOW PARK N6

GRAND JUNCTION PUB,
SOUTH WHARF ROAD W2

Elaborately ornamented
pots, imitating those on
Elizabethan mansions,
were a characteristic
feature of nineteenth
century neo-Elizabethan
buildings; these date
from 1855.

THE LODGE, WATERLOW PARK N6

PANTON STREET SW1

BROMPTON ORATORY SW3

LINCOLN'S INN WC2

218 LAMBETH ROAD SE1

BELL COTTAGE, KYNANCE MEWS W8

SLOANE SQUARE SW1

ALBERT MEMORIAL,
KENSINGTON GARDENS W8

IMPERIAL WAR MUSEUM,
LAMBETH ROAD SE1

100 KENSINGTON HIGH STREET W8

20–22 PONT STREET SW1

22 WATERFORD ROAD SW6

29 MELBURY ROAD W14

HAMMERSMITH HOSPITAL,
DUCANE ROAD W12

84 UPPER TOOTING ROAD SW17

LONDON COLISEUM,
ST MARTIN'S LANE WC2

86–97 KENSINGTON COURT W8

HAMMERSMITH SW13

ROYAL WATERMAN'S SQUARE,
PENGE HIGH STREET SE20

ROYAL MEWS SW1

The pediment, which is the classical elaboration of the gable at the end of a pitched roof, has always provided a setting for symbolic sculpture. William Theed the Elder appropriately sculpted a group with Hercules capturing the Thracian horses for the pediment of the Riding House when Nash refronted it in the 1820s.

SOMERSET HOUSE, LANCASTER PLACE WC2

HANOVER TERRACE NW1

SOUTHWARK SOCIAL SERVICES,
WALWORTH ROAD SE17

46 OLD CHURCH STREET SW3

THE BLACK HORSE AND HARROW,
RUSHEY GREEN SE6

PUBLIC LIBRARY, SPA ROAD SE16

WHITELEYS, QUEENSWAY W2

When Baroness Burdett Coutts commissioned this group of houses from her architect Mr Darbishire, she favoured a thoroughly romantic style, which made great use of the rich shadows thrown by elaborately fretted bargeboards.

HOLLY VILLAGE, SWAINS LANE N6

HARTLEY HALL, FLOWER LANE NW7

THE BUNGALOW, THE RIDGEWAY NW7

3 WOODSIDE LANE N20

THE DURNING LIBRARY, KENNINGTON LANE SE11

40–42 BROOK STREET W1

689 FINCHLEY ROAD NW2

90 HOLLAND ROAD W14

LONDON UNIVERSITY OBSERVATORY, MILL HILL NW7

BRAMLEY AND FRESTON ROADS W11

ST GEORGE'S ROAD SE1

POST OFFICE TOWER W1

GRAY'S INN ROAD AND PENTONVILLE ROAD WC1

THE HIPPODROME, CHARING CROSS ROAD WC2

47–51 DAVIES STREET W1

08 OLD BROMPTON ROAD SW7

ST PANCRAS STATION NW1

63–65 THE CHASE SW4

44 WIGMORE STREET W1

87 OXFORD STREET W1

ISLINGTON HIGH STREET N1

125 CLARENDON ROAD W11

STREATHAM HIGH ROAD SW16

BOROUGH ROAD PUBLIC LIBRARY SE1

BRUNEL ROAD SE16

125 PALL MALL SW1

OLD KENT ROAD SE1

SLOANE SQUARE SW1

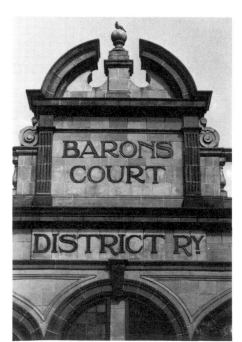

GLIDDON ROAD W14

TOWER BRIDGE EC3

CENTRAL CRIMINAL COURT,
OLD BAILEY EC4

BANK OF ENGLAND,
THREADNEEDLE STREET EC2

67 TOTTENHAM COURT ROAD W1

A gilt copper finial,
simulating a ball of fire,
crowns the Monument,
which was designed by
Christopher Wren in 1671
to commemorate the Great
Fire. The viewing platform
was enclosed by an iron
cage in 1842 to stop suicides.

ST JAMES'S CHURCH, PICCADILLY SW1

ST MARY'S CHURCH,
BATTERSEA CHURCH ROAD SW11

THE MONUMENT EC3

SWEDISH CHURCH,
HARCOURT STREET W1

HAMMERSMITH BRIDGE W6

ST JOHN'S WOOD CHURCH,
WELLINGTON ROAD NW8

70 CONYERS ROAD SW16

ST THOMAS'S HOSPITAL SE1

ROYAL EXCHANGE BUILDING EC3

WALTHAM FOREST TOWN HALL E17

ST ETHELBURGA-THE-VIRGIN WITHIN,
BISHOPSGATE EC3

GRAY'S INN SQUARE WC1

ROYAL HOSPITAL SW3

YOUNG'S BREWERY,
WANDSWORTH HIGH STREET SW18

ST GILES-IN-THE-FIELDS,
HIGH STREET WC2

TEMPLE HOUSE EC4

STAPLE INN EC4

19 CHEYNE PLACE SW3

GREENWICH ROYAL OBSERVATORY SE10

INNER TEMPLE EC4

GUILFORD STREET WC1

EMBANKMENT SW15

ROSENDALE JUNIOR SCHOOL,
TURNEY ROAD SE21

ALL HALLOWS BY THE TOWER,
TOWER PLACE EC3

SUTTON HOSPITAL EC1

224 SHAFTESBURY AVENUE WC2

TRINITY HOUSE, TRINITY SQUARE EC3

LIBERTY'S,
GREAT MARLBOROUGH STREET W1

1 UPPER ST MARTIN'S LANE WC2

SPRINGFIELD METHODIST CHURCH,
WANDSWORTH ROAD SW8

TOOTING PUBLIC LIBRARY SW17

LAMBETH PALACE SE1

BATTERSEA LIBRARY SW11

CHURCH OF ST PHILIP,
EARL'S COURT W8

25–27 WESTLOW STREET SE19

TIME FOR SPORT

7 EALING BROADWAY W5

360 ESSEX ROAD N1

ST ANDREWS, GARRATT LANE SW18

11 JOHN STREET WC1

CHELSEA OLD TOWN HALL, KINGS ROAD SW3

32 NOTTING HILL GATE W2

HOLBORN VIADUCT EC2

123A OLD CHURCH STREET SW3

75 MITCHAM ROAD SW17

THREADNEEDLE STREET EC2

30 BOUVERIE STREET EC4

FLEET STREET EC4

BOUVERIE STREET EC4

HARVEY NICHOLS, KNIGHTSBRIDGE SW1

190 SLOANE STREET SW1

4–5 KING WILLIAM STREET EC4

CHEAPSIDE EC2

15 THEOBALDS ROAD WC1

WHITELEYS, QUEENSWAY W2

ST MAGNUS THE MARTYR, LOWER THAMES STREET EC3

STREATHAM LIBRARY SW16

NORTH END ROAD SW6

ST EDMUND THE KING, LOMBARD STREET EC3

48 GRACECHURCH STREET EC3

ALKIT'S, CAMBRIDGE CIRCUS WC2

108 WANDSWORTH BRIDGE ROAD SW6

41–42 KING WILLIAM STREET EC4

18 HAYMARKET SW1

233 LOWER ROAD SE16

354 STRAND WC2

181 PICCADILLY W1

On the hour Mr Fortnum and Mr Mason come out of their boxes and bow to each other. The grocer and footman to Queen Anne founded this exclusive store in 1707, but the clock was not installed until 1964.

CAMBERWELL NEW ROAD SE5

WILLESDEN JUNCTION NW10

GOSWELL ROAD EC1

COURTS FURNISHING STORE, FALCON ROAD SW11

604 KINGS ROAD SW6

BROCKWELL PARK SE24

PARLIAMENT SQUARE SW1

At midday, this clock doffs its hat high over a gentlemen's outfitter in the Old Kent Road.

HORNIMAN MUSEUM, LONDON ROAD SE23

194 OLD KENT ROAD SE1

Gordon Selfridge started to build his store in 1908, with Daniel Burnham of Chicago as architectural consultant, which accounts for the American feel of the building. The clock is carried by a gigantic figure, 11 feet high, called the 'Queen of Time'.

SELFRIDGES, OXFORD STREET W1

56 NEW OXFORD STREET WC1

3 ENNISMORE MEWS SW7

73 MITCHAM ROAD SW17

SOMERSET HOUSE, LANCASTER PLACE WC2

107 LUDGATE CIRCUS EC4

BRIXTON TOWN HALL SW2

On the hour St George, England's patron saint, pursues the dragon, finally striking it in the neck with his lance.

LIBERTY'S,
GREAT MARLBOROUGH STREET W1

HOOP LANE CREMATORIUM NW11

GUINNESS TRUST BUILDINGS,
DRAYCOTT AVENUE SW3

43 FRITH STREET W1

CANNON STREET EC4

63 SOUTHWARK BRIDGE ROAD SE1

ALLEYN'S SCHOOL,
TOWNLEY ROAD SE22

HAMMERSMITH TUBE STATION W6

CLAPHAM COMMON SW4

GUILFORD STREET WC1

MARE STREET TOWN HALL E8

2 CLAPHAM COMMON NORTH SIDE SW4

MILE END ROAD E1

MARYLEBONE ROAD NW1

ST JOHN'S CHURCH, SMITH SQUARE SW1

ROYAL MEWS SW1

ST JAMES'S PALACE SW1

CHELSEA EMBANKMENT AND OLD CHURCH STREET SW3

29 PECKHAM ROAD SE5

52 CHISWELL STREET EC1

CHURCH ROW SW18

THE TOWER HOTEL E1

51 DEAN STREET W1

96B CORNWALL GARDENS SW7

FINSBURY CIRCUS GARDEN EC2

112 KENSINGTON HIGH STREET W8

10 CLEVELAND PARK AVENUE E17

LIVERPOOL ROAD N1

THE ROEBUCK, KENNINGTON ROAD SE11

440 HORNSEY ROAD N19

UPPER STREET N1

CASTLETON MANSIONS, CLAVERING AVENUE SW13

167 ADELAIDE ROAD NW3

WESTMINSTER CATHEDRAL SW1

John Francis Bentley's marvellous essay in the Byzantine style is incomplete, but these details give ample proof of his outstanding skill.

GOLDSMITHS COLLEGE, LEWISHAM WAY SE14

ACHILLES ROAD NW6

EDWARD ALLEYN HOUSE,
COLLEGE ROAD SE21

ICI HOUSE, SMITH SQUARE SW1

DULWICH COLLEGE SE21

CHESTER TERRACE NW1

SHIPWRIGHT'S ARMS, 86 TOOLEY STREET SE1

WESTMINSTER CATHEDRAL SW1

41 PENGE HIGH STREET SE20

225 EBURY STREET SW1

'Blind' windows intro-
duced into a facade to
balance other openings
have been used since
Elizabethan times, but
their enrichment with
relief panels suggests a
date at the end of the
nineteenth century.

CHEYNE WALK
AND LAWRENCE STREET SW3

GRAND JUNCTION ARMS PUB,
SOUTH WHARF ROAD W2

SAID HOUSE, CHISWICK MALL W4

BARCLAYS BANK, WILLESDEN GREEN BRANCH NW2

HARMWOOD STREET AND CHALK FARM ROAD NW1

GOLDSMITHS' HALL, FOSTER LANE EC2

BRIXTON TOWN HALL SW2

34 SMITH SQUARE SW1

238 WOOD STREET E17

18 BELGRAVE SQUARE SW1

BLACKFRIARS BRIDGE SE1

NEWINGTON LIBRARY AND CUMMING MUSEUM,
WALWORTH ROAD SE17

NEWINGTON LIBRARY AND CUMMING MUSEUM,
WALWORTH ROAD SE17

76 DEPTFORD HIGH STREET SE8

Panels of terracotta or faience tiling allowed very elaborate decorative effects to be reproduced extensively, once the initial model had been carved. These materials enjoyed great popularity from the 1870s till the early 1900s, and were much used on buildings in the Arts and Crafts and Anglo-Dutch styles.

BOROUGH ROAD SE1

159 FRIERN BARNET LANE N20

JUNCTION ROAD N19

23 CAMBERWELL CHURCH STREET SE5

88 ENDYMION ROAD SW2

THE ROSE INN, NEW CROSS ROAD SE14

ROYAL VICTUALLING YARD, GROVE STREET SE8

81 FULHAM ROAD SW3

EVELINA ROAD SE15

THE COUNTY HALL SE1

WATERLOO STATION SE1

The architects Lanchester and Rickards made their building into what is probably the most spectacular example of Edwardian Beaux-Arts baroque in London. It was built between 1905 and 1911.

WESTMINSTER CENTRAL HALL SW1

TRINITY SQUARE EC3

SOUTH BANK HOUSE, LAMBETH HIGH STREET SE1

YE OLDE SPOTTED HORSE, PUTNEY HIGH STREET SW15

7 LOTHBURY EC2

THE COUNTY HALL SE1

STRAND SCHOOL, ELM PARK SW2

DENMARK HOUSE, 15 TOOLEY STREET SE1

27 ALBURY STREET SE8

62–64 GOWER STREET WC1

1–4 HATTON GARDEN EC1

VICTORIA AND ALBERT MUSEUM,
CROMWELL ROAD SW7

NORTH EAST LONDON POLYTECHNIC,
WATER LANE E15

VICTORIA AND ALBERT MUSEUM, EXHIBITION ROAD S

PRUDENTIAL ASSURANCE, HOLBORN BARS EC1

55 BROADWAY SW1

PUBLIC BATHS, PRINCE OF WALES ROAD NW5

Jacob Epstein sculpted the two
large groups for the building which
was completed in 1929. Although
the figures have the lumpy quality
that characterised so much of
Epstein's architectural sculpture,
it is hard to understand the public
outrage which attended most of his
commissions at the time.

GRUMMANT ROAD SE15

11 TUFTON STREET SW1

WANDSWORTH TOWN HALL SW18

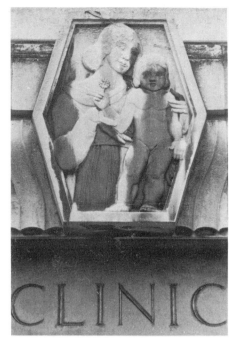

5 DOCK ROAD E1

. WANDSWORTH TOWN HALL SW18

19–21 HATTON GARDEN EC1

GOOD SHEPHERD MISSION, MOSSLEA ROAD SE20

No expense was spared by Sir Frank Baines, when he designed the headquarters in 1928, to enrich the lower levels of the building. The bronze bas-reliefs on the doors commemorate great medical achievements of the past.

ICI HOUSE, MILLBANK SW1

102 OLD BROMPTON ROAD SW7

1 LEATHERMARKET STREET SE1

WANDSWORTH TOWN HALL SW18

NORTH THAMES GAS, THE BROADWAY N8

NEW CHANGE EC4

HORTON HOUSE, MEADOW ROAD SW8

NORTH EAST LONDON POLYTECHNIC,
ROMFORD ROAD, E15

BRIXTON TOWN HALL SW2

DENBIGH ROAD AND CHEPSTOW
VILLAS W11

THE OLD CHERRY TREE PUB,
GROVE VALE SE22

ST JAMES COURT
BUCKINGHAM GATE. SW1

HORNIMAN MUSEUM,
LONDON ROAD SE23

220 ARLINGTON ROAD NW1

NELL GWYNN HOUSE,
SLOANE AVENUE SW3

GREYCOAT HOSPITAL SCHOOL SW1

THE BANQUETING HOUSE,
WHITEHALL SW1

ST MARY ROTHERHITHE, ST MARY CHURCH STREET SE16

13 CLEVELAND PARK AVENUE E17

11 CLEVELAND PARK AVENUE E17

1 CLEVELAND PARK AVENUE E17

440 HORNSEY ROAD N19

THE WHEATSHEAF, 2 UPPER TOOTING ROAD SW17

128 FORTUNE GREEN ROAD NW8

130 WOOD STREET EC2

133–135 PARK ROAD N8

3 FREKE ROAD SW11

5 GROVE ROAD E11

25 QUEEN ANNE'S GATE SW1

NORTH CAMBERWELL LIBRARY SE5

72 ST AGNES PLACE SE11

74 ST AGNES PLACE SE11

BATTERSEA CHURCH STREET SW11

GREAT WESTERN ROYAL HOTEL,
PRAED STREET W2

BLACK FRIAR COURT EC4

SMITH SQUARE SW1

366 KENNINGTON ROAD SE11

11 CHOUMERT ROAD SE15

BLACK FRIAR COURT EC4

23–27 TUDOR STREET EC4

440 HORNSEY ROAD N19

4 GROSVENOR GARDENS SW1

57 PENN ROAD N7

84 ABBEVILLE ROAD SW4

104 MILE END ROAD E1

92 ABBEVILLE ROAD SW4

8 BOUTFLOWER ROAD SW11

AGAMEMNON ROAD NW6

143 UPPER STREET N1

46 ST JOHN'S HILL GROVE SW11

2 COPLESTON ROAD SE15

136 PUTNEY HIGH STREET SW15

The Red Indian heads were introduced onto the stucco keystones when two houses were united to form the American Embassy residence of Sir Joseph Kennedy in the 1930s.

14 PRINCE'S GATE SW7

THE RAILWAY HOTEL, PUTNEY HIGH STREET SW15

HORNIMAN LODGE, HORNIMAN GARDENS SE23

THE ANGERSTEIN HOTEL, WOOLWICH ROAD SE10

OLD KINGS HEAD, BEAR STREET WC2

'SUNNYFIELD', WEST HEATH ROAD NW3

21 DURAND GARDENS SW9

57 TUFTON STREET SW1

The entrance to the churchyard of St Olave's with these skulls above was referred to by Charles Dickens in *The Uncommercial Traveller*, as the entrance to 'the churchyard of St Ghastly Grim'.

ST OLAVE'S CHURCH, SEETHING LANE EC3

59 KENNINGTON ROAD SE1

1 UPPER ST MARTIN'S LANE WC2

FLANNIGAN'S TOWER PUB,
SELBOURNE ROAD E17

40 TABARD STREET SE1

NORWEGIAN CHURCH,
ALBION STREET SE11

THE OLD QUEENS HEAD,
STOCKWELL ROAD SW9

TRYON STREET SW3

113 CLAPHAM COMMON NORTH SIDE SW4

2 MARGRAVINE GARDENS W14

MARY DATCHELOR SCHOOL,
CAMBERWELL GROVE SE5

Male caryatids are known
as atlantes, but they have
never been as popular as
the females.

48 NEWINGTON CAUSEWAY SE1

HAMMERSMITH TOWN HALL W6

39 SOUTHWARK BRIDGE ROAD SE1

ALFRED THE GREAT,
TRINITY CHURCH SQUARE SE1

EDWARD VII, MILE END ROAD E1

EDWARD VII, TOOTING BROADWAY SW17

QUEEN VICTORIA,
KENSINGTON GARDENS W8

QUEEN VICTORIA, THE MALL SW1

PRINCE ALBERT, HOLBORN CIRCUS EC1

CHARLES II, SOHO SQUARE W1

CHARLES I, TRAFALGAR SQUARE WC2

This fine equestrian sculpture by Le Sueur, made in 1633, was obviously based on the European precedent set by the statues of Cosimo de Medici in Florence and Henri IV on the Pont Neuf in Paris.

PRINCE ALBERT,
KENSINGTON GARDENS W8

JAMES II, TRAFALGAR SQUARE WC2

QUEEN ANNE, QUEEN ANNE'S GATE SW1

RICHARD I, OLD PALACE YARD SW1

GEORGE IV, TRAFALGAR SQUARE WC2

GEORGE VI, THE MALL SW1

GEORGE V, ST MARGARET STREET SW1

SAMUEL JOHNSON,
ST CLEMENT DANE'S CHURCHYARD WC2

GEORGE IV, PRINCE REGENT PUB,
DULWICH ROAD SE24

PAUL JULIUS REUTER,
ROYAL EXCHANGE BUILDINGS EC 2

ST GEORGE, ST JOHN'S WOOD ROAD
AND PRINCE ALBERT ROAD NW8

SIGMUND FREUD,
SWISS COTTAGE LIBRARY NW3

EDWARD VII, WATERLOO PLACE SW1

WALTER RALEIGH, WHITEHALL SW1

WILLIAM EWART GLADSTONE,
BOW ROAD E3

WINSTON CHURCHILL,
PARLIAMENT SQUARE SW1

KARL MARX, HIGHGATE CEMETERY N6

ROBERT BURNS, VICTORIA
EMBANKMENT GARDENS WC2

CAPTAIN COOK, THE MALL, SW1

GENERAL WOLFE,
GREENWICH PARK SE10

SIR THOMAS MORE,
CHELSEA EMBANKMENT SW3

GEORGE WASHINGTON,
TRAFALGAR SQUARE WC2

WILLIAM BOOTH, MILE END ROAD E1

FIELD-MARSHAL EARL ROBERTS,
HORSE GUARDS PARADE SW1

ROBERT FALCON SCOTT
WATERLOO PLACE SW1

SIR JOHN FRANKLIN,
WATERLOO PLACE SW1

SPHINX, VICTORIA EMBANKMENT WC2

ARTHUR SULLIVAN, VICTORIA
EMBANKMENT GARDENS WC2

BASE OF SULLIVAN STATUE, VICTORIA EMBANKMENT GARDENS WC2

WILLIAM HUSKISSON,
GROSVENOR GARDENS SW1

SIR ROBERT PEEL,
PARLIAMENT SQUARE SW1

JOHN F. KENNEDY,
MARYLEBONE ROAD W1

ISAMBARD KINGDOM BRUNEL,
VICTORIA EMBANKMENT GARDENS WC2

PETER PAN, KENSINGTON GARDENS W2

DAVID, CHELSEA EMBANKMENT SW3

OLIVER CROMWELL,
PARLIAMENT SQUARE SW1

ABRAHAM LINCOLN,
PARLIAMENT SQUARE SW1

THE ATHENAEUM,
WATERLOO PLACE SW1

The gilded statue of Athena, the goddess of wisdom, which stands on the portico was sculpted by Baily in 1850. Behind her can be seen a part of the reproduction of the Parthenon frieze which runs round the building. A wit wrote of the club's promoter:
'I'm John Wilson Croker
I do as I please.
They wanted an Ice House,
I gave them a frieze'

EROS, PICCADILLY CIRCUS W1

BOADICEA, WESTMINSTER BRIDGE SW1

THE MALL SW1

BURGHERS OF CALAIS, VICTORIA TOWER GARDENS SW1

CUTTY SARK, GREENWICH SE10

PADDINGTON STREET W1

THOMAS GUY, GUYS HOSPITAL SE1

LANCASTER GATE W2

ALBERT MEMORIAL,
KENSINGTON GARDENS W8

GLOUCESTER GATE NW1

REGENTS PARK NW1

10 TRINITY SQUARE EC3

HOLBORN VIADUCT EC1

CADOGAN PLACE SW1

31 ISLINGTON GREEN N1

POCAHONTAS, RED LION SQUARE WC1

HOSPITAL FOR SICK CHILDREN,
GREAT ORMOND STREET WC1

When the Inwoods (father and son) built their masterpiece in 1819–22 they were so committed to neo-classicism as to raise a copy of the Erechtheum porch from the Acropolis in Athens on top of the vestry. They did improve on the original caryatids however in that they replaced the arms and hands which are missing in Athens.

ST PANCRAS PARISH CHURCH EUSTON ROAD NW1

25 OLD BOND STREET W1

43 HATTON GARDEN EC1

43 HATTON GARDEN EC1

CHALTON STREET NW1

SIR JOHN CASS'S FOUNDATION
SCHOOL EC3

SIR JOHN CASS'S FOUNDATION
SCHOOL EC3

WATERLOW PARK N6

Below Lord Palmerston
insisted that George Gilbert
Scott's new Foreign Office
building should be in the
classical style, instead of
the gothic that Scott
favoured. The result, built
over many years, but mostly
between 1858 and 1874, is
one of the most impressive
of all purpose-built
government offices.

GUILD CHURCH OF ST ANDREW,
HOLBORN EC1

GUILD CHURCH OF ST ANDREW,
HOLBORN EC1

VINTNERS' PLACE EC4

WHITEHALL SW1

MARKS AND SPENCER,
EDGWARE ROAD W2

'BERMONDSEY BOY' (TOMMY STEELE),
ALBION STREET SE16

VICTORIA EMBANKMENT GARDENS WC2

BATTERSEA PARK SW11

HORSE GUARDS ROAD SW1

GROSVENOR GARDENS SW1

FLORENCE NIGHTINGALE,
WATERLOO PLACE SW1

FLORENCE NIGHTINGALE,
ST THOMAS' HOSPITAL SE1

DUKE OF WELLINGTON,
HYDE PARK CORNER W1

CRIMEA WAR MEMORIAL, WATERLOO PLACE SW1

HORATIO NELSON,
TRAFALGAR SQUARE WC2

CRIMEA WAR MEMORIAL,
WATERLOO PLACE SW1

HORSE GUARDS PARADE SW1

TURNEY ROAD SE21

VAUXHALL MANOR SCHOOL SW8

67 BOROUGH HIGH STREET SE1

TURNEY ROAD SE21

PECKHAM PARK ROAD SE15

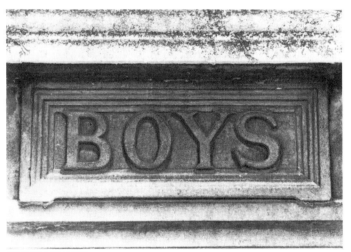

TURNEY ROAD SE21

HACKFORD ROAD SW9

WILSON ROAD SE5

SOUTH WHARF ROAD W2

STANHOPE GARDENS SW7

48 COMMERCIAL ROAD E1

66 VENN STREET SW4

16 OSTADE ROAD SW2

1–17 PEEL STREET W8

CAMBERWELL NEW ROAD SE5

BATHS

PRINCE OF WALES ROAD NW5

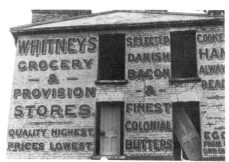

OAKVALE ROAD SE15

67 MONMOUTH STREET WC2

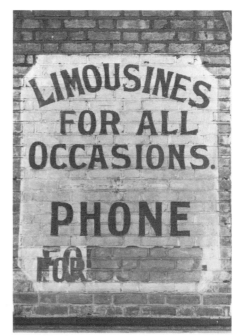

182 LORDSHIP LANE SE22

CHRIST'S CHAPEL, DULWICH COLLEGE SE21

Below The ancient lights notice reinforces the owner's claim to have enjoyed his present amount of natural light for a minimum of twenty years, and his consequent right to continue to do so.

40 SMITH SQUARE SW1

48 OLD GLOUCESTER STREET WC1

ROMAN WAY N7

LYHAM ROAD SW2

214 NORWOOD ROAD SE24

CAMDEN ROAD NW1

HIGH STREET E17

PEABODY ESTATE SE24

PEABODY ESTATE SE24

PEABODY ESTATE SE24

PALACE GARDENS TERRACE W8

VICTORIA STATION SW1

GARFORD STREET E14

EARLS COURT ROAD SW5

12 SYMONS STREET SW3

11 WEST INDIA DOCK ROAD E14

19 NORWOOD HIGH STREET SE27

HAMMERSMITH BRIDGE ROAD W14

12 BLACKHEATH VILLAGE SE3

PARKWAY AND ARLINGTON
ROADS NW1

ELDER AVENUE AND BROADWAY
PARADE N8

110 HOLLAND PARK AVENUE W11

ROMNEY STREET SW1

THE FRENCH INSTITUTE SW7

THE FRENCH INSTITUTE SW7

40 FORTUNE GREEN ROAD NW6

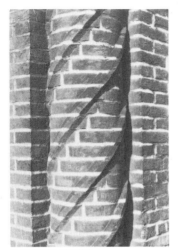

SOMERS PLACE SW2

1 THORNTON AVENUE SW2

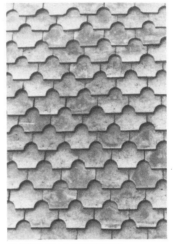

2A WADHAM GARDENS NW3

56 ELMBOURNE ROAD SW17

GREAT GUILFORD STREET SE1

12 MEADWAY NW11

ST JOHN AND ST ELIZABETH HOSPITAL,
CIRCUS ROAD NW8

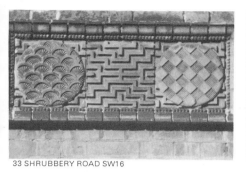

33 SHRUBBERY ROAD SW16

84 ENDYMION ROAD SW2

4 HOLNE CHASE N2

HIGH ROAD N20

47 HEYFORD AVENUE SW8

34 CROFTDOWN ROAD NW5

31 SHRUBBERY ROAD SW16

43 HEYFORD AVENUE SW8

40 THURLOW PARK ROAD SE21

Carved or moulded brickwork was popular as far back as Elizabethan times, but the practice underwent a revival in the late nineteenth century.

507 GARRATT LANE SW18

28 SPENCER ROAD SW18

62 CRYSTAL PALACE PARK ROAD SE26

84 ENDYMION ROAD SW2

19 SYDENHAM ROAD SE26

6 CHEPSTOW ROAD W2

18 HAYMARKET SW1

40 ST MARTIN'S LANE WC2

9 TRANQUIL VALE SE3

3 BUCKINGHAM GATE SW1

21 BRUTON STREET W1

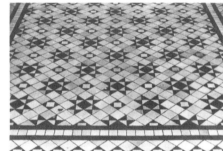

59 DOUGHTY STREET WC1

54 BOROUGH HIGH STREET SE1

129 MOUNT STREET W1

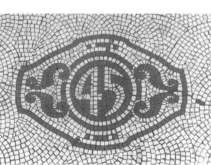

45 GOWER STREET WC1

48 GREEK STREET W1

113 HARLEY STREET W1

13–24 OLD BROMPTON ROAD SW5

25 BEDFORD SQUARE WC1

20–22 MADDOX STREET W1

THE ENTERPRISE, CROGSLAND ROAD NW1

GASBOARD PERRY HILL SE6

THE FLASK, FLASK LANE NW3

CALEDONIAN ROAD STATION N7

GOOSE AND FIRKIN,
BOROUGH ROAD SE1

81 FULHAM ROAD SW3

38 PARKHURST ROAD N7

3 LACY STREET SW15

THE ROSE AND CROWN, OLD TOWN SW4

MICHELIN BUILDING SW7

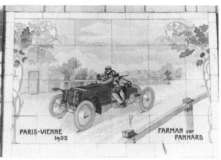

MICHELIN BUILDING SW7

The tile panels on the outside of the building, hand-made by Gilardoni Fils et Cie of Paris, make up a remarkable record of early motor racing. They were installed when François Espinasse, who had designed the original building in 1905, extended the premises in 1910-11.

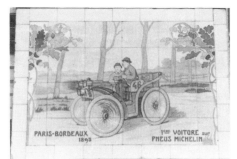

MICHELIN BUILDING SW7

MICHELIN BUILDING SW7

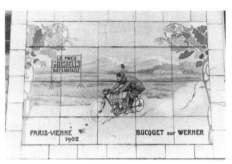

MICHELIN BUILDING SW7

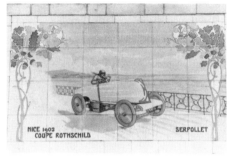

MICHELIN BUILDING SW7

MICHELIN BUILDING SW7

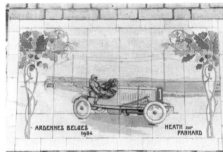

MICHELIN BUILDING SW7

MICHELIN BUILDING SW7

MICHELIN BUILDING SW7

MICHELIN BUILDING SW7

MICHELIN BUILDING SW7

WINCHESTER SQUARE SE1

SCOUT LANE SW4

GRAY'S INN WC1

209 WOOD STREET E17

SOUTHWARK CATHEDRAL SE1

HORNIMAN GARDENS, LONDON ROAD SE23

GRAY'S INN PLACE WC1

GOLDERS GREEN BUS STATION NW11

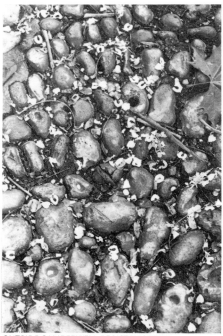
OUTSIDE CAMBERWELL REGISTRY OFFICE,
PECKHAM ROAD SE5

CHESTER CLOSE SW1

SOMERSET HOUSE, LANCASTER PLACE WC2

STAPLE INN EC4

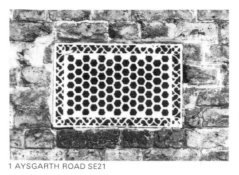

1 AYSGARTH ROAD SE21

194 BRYNMAER ROAD SW11

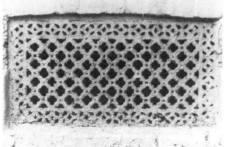

183 BOW ROAD E3

ETLOE HOUSE, CHURCH ROAD E10

ABOVE PUBLIC LAVATORIES,
TOOTING BROADWAY SW17

CORONATION BUILDINGS, SOUTH LAMBETH ROAD SW8

WESTMINSTER ARMS PUB, MARSHAM STREET SW1

NORTH SQUARE NW11

100 TORRIANO AVENUE NW5

193 EUSTON ROAD NW1

SOMERS PLACE SW2

DEPTFORD BROADWAY SE8

9 HYDE PARK GATE SW7

92 NORTH ROAD N6

14 PRINCE'S GATE SW7

Places with interesting historical associations are marked with a blue plaque by the Greater London Council (GLC) and before that by the London County Council (LCC). There are over 350 such plaques in London.

22 THEOBALDS ROAD WC1

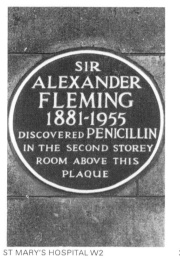

ST MARY'S HOSPITAL W2

27A MILE END ROAD E1

13 HOBART PLACE SW1

116 UPPER STREET N1

LANSDOWNE RISE W11

DRAYCOTT AVENUE SW3

UNITY HOUSE, EUSTON ROAD NW1

56 TITE STREET SW3

51 GLEBE PLACE SW3

459 KINGS ROAD SW3

CLOAK LANE EC4

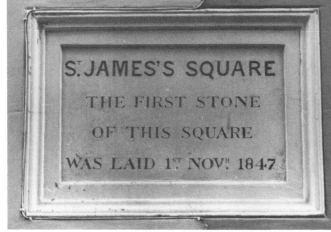

1 ST JAMES'S GARDENS W11

CHURCHROW HOUSES SW18

Firemarks, small metallic plaques on buildings, were issued by insurance companies to advertise that the recipient was insured with them against fire. If the house was not insured, the fire engines, then privately owned, would not turn out.

GUYS HOSPITAL SE1

WHITE LION STREET N1

WOOLWICH ROAD LIBRARY SE2

EVELINA MANSIONS
CAMBERWELL ROAD SE5

40 MUSEUM STREET WC1

62 LOMBARD STREET EC3

241 WALWORTH ROAD SE11

27 LEATHER LANE EC1

The three gilded balls hanging outside pawnbrokers' premises are related to the device on the coat of arms of the Medici family, the greatest financiers and money lenders of the Italian Renaissance.

15 LOMBARD STREET EC3

WARWICK LANE EC4

THE · MOTHERS UNION

24 TUFTON STREET SW1

54 LOMBARD STREET EC3

68 KING WILLIAM STREET EC4

6 EDEN ROAD E17

152 HIGH STREET E17

33 CATHERINE STREET WC2

TRAFALGAR SQUARE WC2

3 BURLINGTON GARDENS W1

74 CHARLOTTE STREET W1

74 HIGH STREET W8

53 NEW OXFORD STREET WC1

3 MOXON STREET W1

3 GERRARD STREET W1

5 BOUTFLOWER ROAD SW11

185 WESTBOURNE GROVE W2

41 KENSINGTON HIGH STREET W8

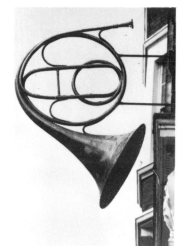

116 LONG ACRE WC2

78 NEAL STREET WC2

STANDISH ROAD
AND THERESA ROAD W6

599 FULHAM ROAD SW6

GOLDBEATERS HOUSE,
MANETTE STREET W1

21A JERMYN STREET SW1

67 LOMBARD STREET EC3

83 LAMB'S CONDUIT STREET WC1

PENTONVILLE ROAD N1

89 PORTOBELLO ROAD W11

10 FELKIRK ROAD SW17

178 UPPER TOOTING ROAD SW17

196 TOTTENHAM COURT ROAD W1

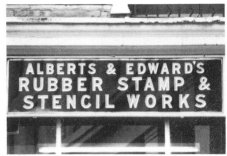

16 CREECHURCH LANE EC3

LIBERTY'S, GREAT MARLBOROUGH STREET W1

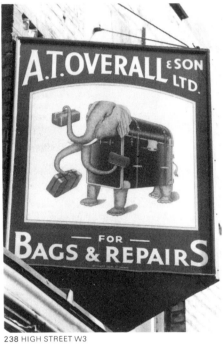

238 HIGH STREET W3

1 WESTMORELAND ROAD SE17

182 DRURY LANE WC2

23 CHARLOTTE STREET W1

93 STRAND WC2

46 GREAT RUSSELL STREET WC1

71 JERMYN STREET SW1

ROYAL EXCHANGE BUILDINGS EC2

105 DARTMOUTH ROAD SE23

54 BOROUGH HIGH STREET SE1

38 LOMBARD STREET EC3

80–81 LOWER MARSH SE1

45 ALBEMARLE STREET W1

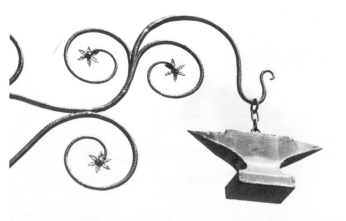

62 LOMBARD STREET EC3

194 OLD KENT ROAD SE1

PEMBROKE MEWS W8

BALHAM STATION ROAD SW12

496 NEW CROSS ROAD SE14

412 GARRATT LANE SW18

8 NEW BOND STREET W1

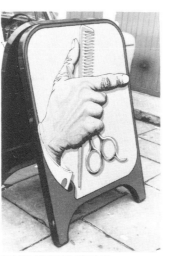

350 CALEDONIAN ROAD N1

111 TRAFALGAR ROAD SE10

71 CROSS STREET N1

131 SOUTH LAMBETH ROAD SW8

132 BROOK DRIVE SE11

51 MUSEUM STREET WC1

PARKGATE ROAD SW11

CADOGAN PLACE SW1

SOHO SQUARE W1

OLD PALACE YARD SW1

ST JAMES'S PALACE SW1

WILTON ROW SW1

Near the Tower of London is the entrance to what was the first tube railway in the world. Constructed in 1869–70 by the engineer P W Barlow, it conveyed passengers under the Thames from Tower Hill to Tooley Street.

TOWER HILL EC3

GLOUCESTER GATE, REGENTS PARK NW1

KENSINGTON GARDENS W8

TRAFALGAR SQUARE WC2

KENSINGTON GARDENS W8

RUSKIN PARK SE5

HAYMARKET SW1

One of the few genuine late eighteenth century shopfronts still in use, and probably the most famous in London. Commercial pressures and changes have brought about their destruction, though a few are still to be found in old suburbs like Spitalfields.

66 AMWELL STREET EC1

97 EVELINA ROAD SE15

431 HACKNEY ROAD E2

181 MANOR PLACE SE17

82 UPPER STREET N1

739 COMMERCIAL ROAD E14

50 KENNINGTON ROAD SE1

95 ESSEX ROAD N1

STONE HOUSE COURT EC2

2 BEAUCHAMP PLACE SW3

35 CONWAY STREET W1

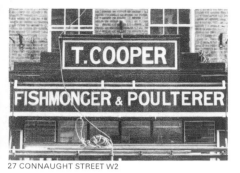

27 CONNAUGHT STREET W2

313 EUSTON ROAD NW1

344 CALEDONIAN ROAD N1

253 WEST END LANE NW6

1 BEADON ROAD W6

KNIGHTSBRIDGE SW1

A good example of a late Victorian provision shop; the whole of the front can be opened as one gigantic sliding sash window.

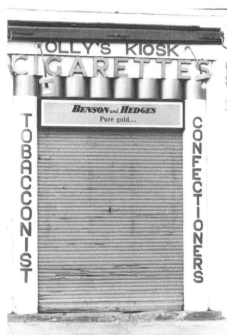

NORTH END ROAD SW6

12 SYMONS STREET SW3

131 SOUTH LAMBETH ROAD SW8

89 CLERKENWELL ROAD EC1

GREAT ORMOND STREET WC1

68 DEAN STREET W1

235 BROMPTON ROAD SW3

99 FALCON ROAD SW11

78 LONG ACRE WC2

ST SWITHIN'S LANE EC4

74 DALLING ROAD W4

POLLOCKS TOY MUSEUM, WHITFIELD STREET W1

7 MILNER STREET SW3

74 CHARING CROSS ROAD WC2

VIRGIN RECORDS, LADBROKE GROVE W11

155 BRICK LANE E2

197 UPPER STREET N1

PORTSMOUTH STREET WC2

412 GARRATT LANE SW18

BURLINGTON ARCADE W1

45 GREENWICH CHURCH STREET SE10

KINGSWAY WC2

65 GOLBORNE ROAD W10

426 COLDHARBOUR LANE SW9

OLD BROAD STREET EC2

20 WESTOW HILL SE19

127 QUEENSWAY W2

288 CALEDONIAN ROAD N1

46 UPPER TOOTING ROAD SW17

53 NEW OXFORD STREET WC1

110 HOLLAND PARK AVENUE W11

28 ENGLANDS LANE NW3

483 GARRATT LANE SW18

28 NEW ROW WC2

6 WOBURN WALK WC1

148 BLACK PRINCE ROAD SE11

285 CALEDONIAN ROAD N1

66 KENSINGTON CHURCH STREET W8

28 CONNAUGHT STREET W2

3 MONTPELIER STREET SW3

5 HARRINGTON ROAD SW7

Children are Not Allowed to Play Beyond This Point.

ST JOHN'S WOOD CHURCHYARD,
WELLINGTON PLACE NW8

The 'Roman' Bath

OPEN DAILY
10 a.m. to 12·30 p.m.
EXCEPT
Sundays, Christmas Day and
Good Friday

ADMISSION
Free

SURREY STEPS WC2

DUKE ·of· YORK'S
HEADQUARTERS

KINGS ROAD SW3

NOTICE

ALLOTMENT ACT, 1922.

This Land is cultivated as garden
allotments. Any person who without
lawful authority or by negligence,
causes

DAMAGE

to any Allotment Garden, growing
crops, fences or buildings thereon, is
liable, on summary conviction to a
fine of

£5

ISSUED BY THE
NATIONAL ALLOTMENTS SOCIETY, LIMITED
DRAYTON HOUSE, GORDON STREET, LONDON, W.C.1.

ROSENDALE ROAD SE21

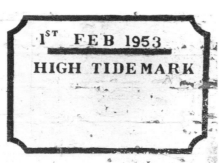

1ST FEB 1953

HIGH TIDE MARK

EMBANKMENT SW15

TRADESMEN'S
ENTRANCE

91 EATON PLACE SW1

BOROUGH OF HAMPSTEAD
THIS TREE WAS PLANTED BY THE MAYOR,
Mr ALDERMAN C.F. PRITCHARD.
· 20TH DECEMBER 1902 ·
IN COMMEMORATION OF THE CORONATION OF
HIS MAJESTY KING EDWARD VII.

FORTUNE GREEN, WEST END LANE NE6

CHRISTIANS
ENQUIRIES

SHAD THAMES SE1

THE HEALTH
OF THE PEOPLE IS
THE HIGHEST LAW

SOUTHWARK SOCIAL SERVICES,
WALWORTH ROAD SE17

JUDGES
ENTRANCE

LAMBETH COUNTY COURT, CLEAVER STREET SE11

PRIME MERIDIAN
OF THE WORLD

EAST | WEST
LONGITUDE | LONGITUDE

Centre of transit circle
Latitude   51° 28' 38" North
Longitude   0° 0' 00"

GREENWICH ROYAL OBSERVATORY SE10

CORNWALL GARDENS SW7

DULWICH PARK SE21

BROCKWELL PARK SE24

CHALCOT ROAD NW3

MARE STREET E8

48 HOOP LANE NW11

LEICESTER SQUARE GARDENS WC2

PARKER MEWS WC2

2 WADHAM GARDENS NW3

A very rare leftover from World
War II, when such signs were
to be found in almost every street
in London.

VICTORIA EMBANKMENT GARDENS WC2

16 LORD NORTH STREET SW1

JOCKEY'S FIELDS, GRAY'S INN WC1

LORD'S CRICKET GROUND NW8

ROSENDALE ROAD SE24

LONG LANE EC1

BETWEEN 33 & 35 INGRAM AVENUE NW11

NEW CROSS BATHS SE14

FRANKHAM STREET SE8

CROXTED ROAD AND TURNEY ROAD SE21

THAMES ROAD W4

WESTERN HOSPITAL SW6

8 BATTERSEA PARK ROAD SW11

176 EBURY STREET SW1

PICCADILLY CIRCUS W1

ALDGATE STATION,
WHITECHAPEL HIGH STREET E1

BETHNAL GREEN ROAD E2

OUTSIDE 248 WEST END LANE NW6

JEBB AVENUE SW2

FELSHAM ROAD SW15

COKERS LANE SE21

HOOP LANE AND FINCHLEY ROAD NW11

MARE STREET BUS STATION E8

GLENEAGLE ROAD SW16

EAST DULWICH GROVE SE22

THROGMORTON AVENUE EC2

4 GARWAY ROAD W2

LOOK BOTH WAYS BEFORE CROSSING ROAD

KEYWORTH STREET SE1

THERE IS NO RIGHT OF WAY THROUGH THE CHURCHYARD BUT YOU ARE WELCOME TO USE THE PATHS. PLEASE TAKE YOUR LITTER AWAY

STREATHAM HIGH ROAD SW16

GREATER LONDON COUNCIL KEEP OFF THESE WALLS AND ROOFS ARE TREATED WITH ANTI-CLIMB PAINT.

HORLE WALK, LOUGHBOROUGH ROAD SW9

YOU MAY TELEPHONE FROM HERE

THE CRICKETERS, NEWINGTON BUTTS SE11

PRIVATE ROAD HEAVY VEHICLES FUNERALS & HAWKERS PROHIBITED

PALACE ROAD SW2

TO THE PUBLIC BATHS AND WASH-HOUSES CHESHIRE STREET

OPPOSITE 109 BETHNAL GREEN ROAD E2

YOUR MITE MEANS MUCH TO ST BARNABAS

ST BARNABAS CHURCH SW1

HALT BEWARE OF PEDESTRIANS

165 HOE STREET E17

TO THE LADIES LAVATORY

PUTNEY HIGH STREET SW15

WOMAN

NORTH CAMBERWELL LIBRARY SE5

DECENCY FORBIDS Lavatory Opposite

123 BAYSWATER ROAD W2

GENTLEMEN

WEST END LANE NW6

MEN

NEW CROSS BATHS SE14

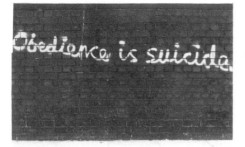

KILBURN PRIORY NW6

KILBURN PRIORY NW6

AMEN CORNER SW17

59 GREAT SUFFOLK STREET SE1

ST LUKE'S, NORWOOD HIGH STREET SE27

KENNINGTON PARK ROAD SE11

44A SYDENHAM ROAD SE26

GARRATT LANE SW18

OVAL CRICKET GROUND SE11

GREAT GUILDFORD STREET SE1

35–37 SOUTHWARK BRIDGE ROAD SE1

DUNBAR STREET SE27

BELSIZE GROVE NW3

NINE ELMS LANE SW8

CAMBERWELL ROAD SE5

133 LOWER RICHMOND ROAD SW15

ANCHOR MISSION HALL
GARRATT LANE SW18

STREATHAM HIGH ROAD SW16

MOUNTAIN HOUSE, JONATHAN STREET SE11

CRYSTAL PALACE STATION SE19

MITCHAM ROAD SW17

STREATHAM VALE SW16

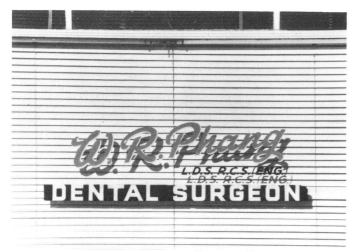

360A KING STREET W6

THE CAMBRIDGE SE19

ALLEYN PARK SE21

BATTERSEA PARK SW11

1 PEARDON STREET SW8

47 PECKHAM PARK ROAD SE15

CRYSTAL PALACE PARK SE19

WHITECHAPEL ROAD E1

BETHNAL GREEN ROAD E2

1 BANKSIDE SE1

RED LION STREET WC1

1 BANKSIDE SE1

WAPPING WALL E1

DOCK STREET E1

ACRE LANE SW2

HACKNEY ROAD E2

PARK ROW SE10   102 OLD BROMPTON ROAD SW7

THE PRINCE OF WALES,
BRIXTON ROAD SW2

SALTWELL STREET E14

THE SWAN, DEPTFORD HIGH STREET SE8

SUGAR LOAF WALK E2

GOOSE AND FIRKIN,
BOROUGH ROAD SE1

THE MASONS ARMS,
BATTERSEA PARK ROAD SW8

SMUGGLERS TAVERN,
28 WARREN STREET W1

174 CAMBERWELL ROAD SE5

BRIXTON ROAD SW9

THE DUKE OF CLARENCE, VAUXHALL BRIDGE ROAD SW1

GARRATT LANE SW18

RYE LANE SE15

STOKE NEWINGTON
CHURCH STREET N16

157 BRICK LANE E2

489 LIVERPOOL ROAD N1

THE RAM, YORK ROAD SW18

799 OLD KENT ROAD SE15

HAVERSTOCK HILL NW3

THE RAM, YORK ROAD SW18

THE ROSE AND CROWN, OLD TOWN SW4

96 NEWINGTON CAUSEWAY SE1

VICTORIA STREET SW1

COMMERCIAL STREET E1

MILE END ROAD E1

22 FLEET STREET EC4

98 FETTER LANE EC4

WILTON MEWS SW1

CATHERINE STREET WC2

LUDGATE HILL EC4

THE BREWMASTER,
37 CRANBOURN STREET WC2

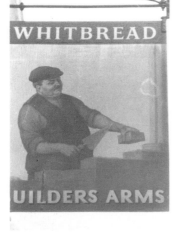

ST PAUL'S ROAD N1

UPPER TULSE HILL SW2

SHAKESPEARE'S HEAD
29 GREAT MARLBOROUGH STREET W1

FORTUNE GREEN ROAD NW8

CHANCERY LANE WC2

CLERKENWELL ROAD EC1

25 LITCHFIELD STREET WC2

BATTERSEA HIGH STREET SW11

392 KINGS ROAD SW3

CHARTERHOUSE STREET EC1

28 SOUTH MOLTON STREET W1

HACKNEY ROAD E2

44 UPPER STREET N1

NORTH END ROAD NW11

THE FIVE BELLS,
NEW CROSS ROAD SE14

UPPER STREET N1

BOROUGH ROAD SE1

THE WHEATSHEAF,
2 UPPER TOOTING ROAD SW17

THE RISING SUN, HIGH WOOD HILL NW7

THE CASTLE,
PUTNEY BRIDGE ROAD SW15

96 DEAN STREET W1

97 TOOLEY STREET SE1

WINE OFFICE COURT EC4

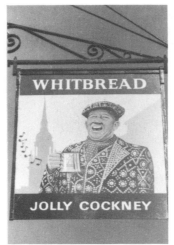

BLACK PRINCE ROAD SE11

WOOD STREET E17

WHITECHAPEL ROAD E1

459 KINGS ROAD SW3

150 WARWICK ROAD W8

LAMBETH ROAD SE1

WOODGRANGE ROAD E7

WILFRED STREET SW11

DEVONSHIRE ROAD SE23

THE GOLDEN FLEECE, LAW STREET SE1

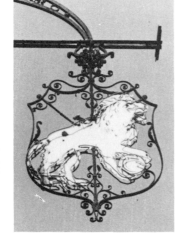

THE WHITE LION,
STREATHAM HIGH ROAD SW16

4 NEW KING STREET SE8

185 PICCADILLY W1

ROYAL VETERINARY COLLEGE NW1

VESTRY ROAD SORTING OFFICE E17

QUEEN'S ARMS, WESTON HILL SE19

GATLIFF ROAD SW1

HARRODS, KNIGHTSBRIDGE SW3

185 PICCADILLY W1

143 NEW BOND STREET W1

STREATHAM SORTING OFFICE, PRENTIS ROAD SW16

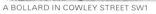

A BOLLARD IN COWLEY STREET SW1

BRIXTON TOWN HALL SW2

TRINITY GREEN, MILE END ROAD E1

POLYTECHNIC OF THE SOUTH BANK SE1

CAMBERWELL CEMETERY,
BRENCHLEY GARDENS SE23

THE COUNTY HALL SE1

UNION OF POST OFFICE WORKERS,
CRESCENT LANE SW4

E. AYLING AND SONS, EMBANKMENT SW15

MUNICIPAL BUILDING, WANDSWORTH HIGH STREET SW18

HAMMERSMITH SW13

SOUTHEY ROAD SW9

TOWNLEY ROAD SE22

ROYAL NAVAL COLLEGE SE10

47 GREAT MARLBOROUGH STREET W1

WADHAM ROAD NW3

GREENWICH SE10

101 QUEEN VICTORIA STREET EC4

BOILEAU ARMS, CASTELNAU SW13

17 HENRIETTA STREET WC2

MUNICIPAL BUILDINGS,
WANDSWORTH HIGH STREET SW18

CITY AND GUILDS ART SCHOOL SE11

MUNICIPAL BUILDINGS, WANDSWORTH HIGH STREET SW18

75 MITCHAM ROAD SW17

GUYS HOSPITAL SE1

13 ST SWITHIN'S LANE EC4

BURBAGE ROAD SE21

SOUTHWARK CATHEDRAL SE1

88 WHITECHAPEL ROAD E1